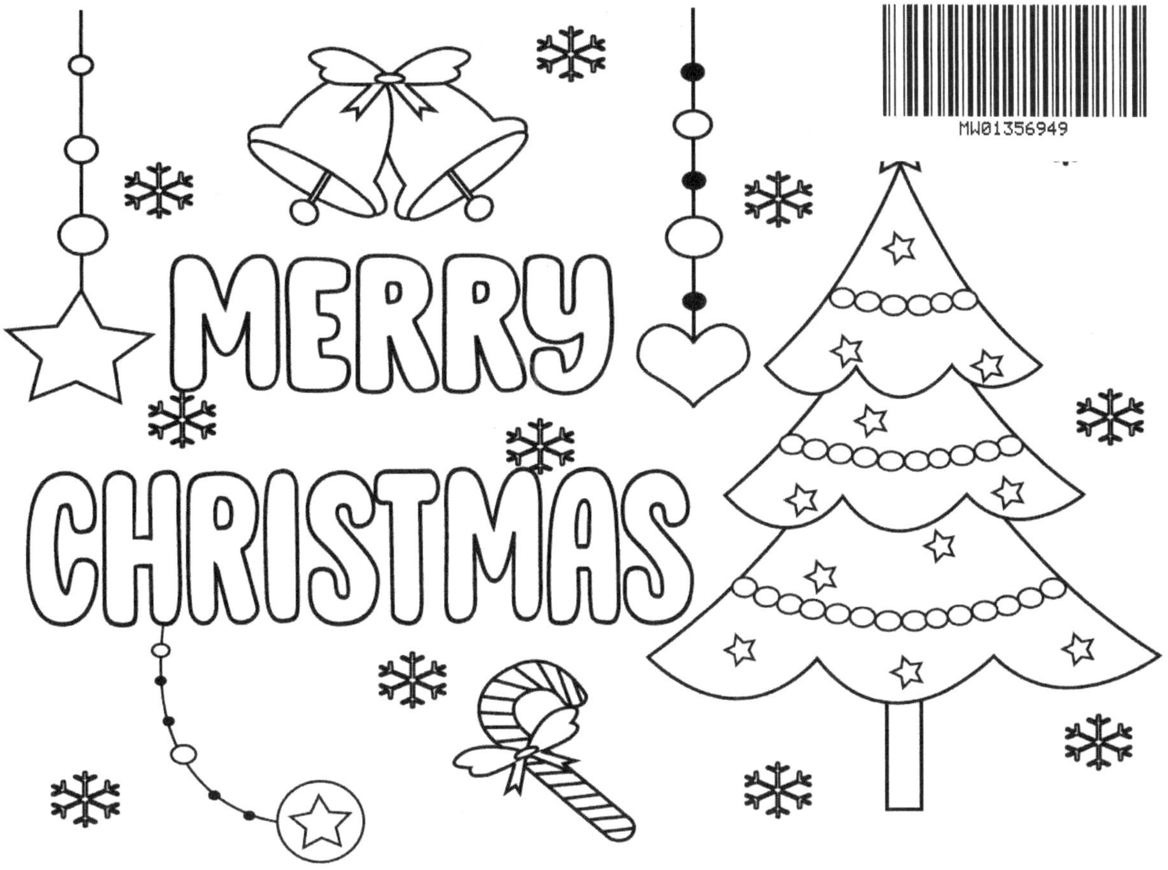

This Book Belongs To...

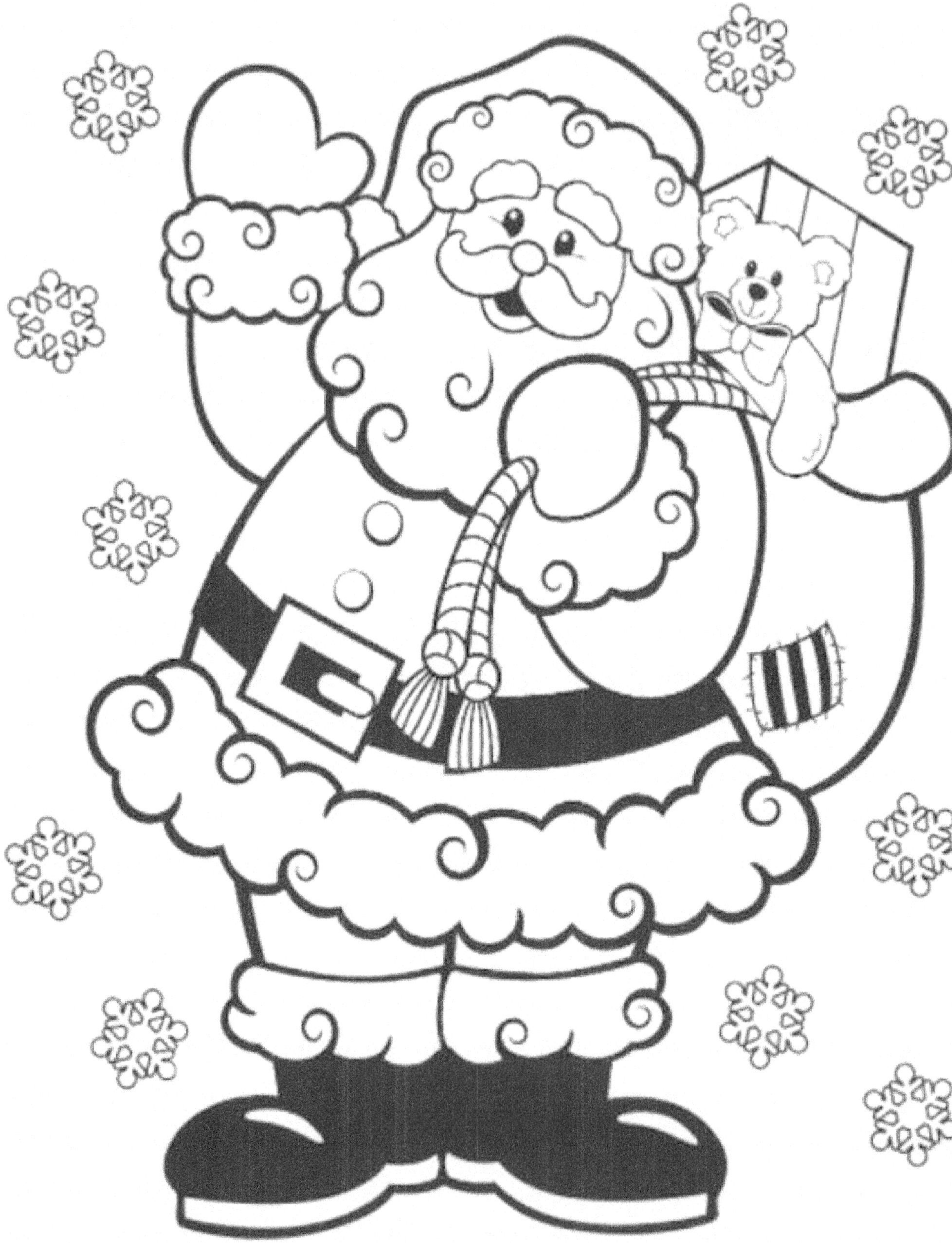

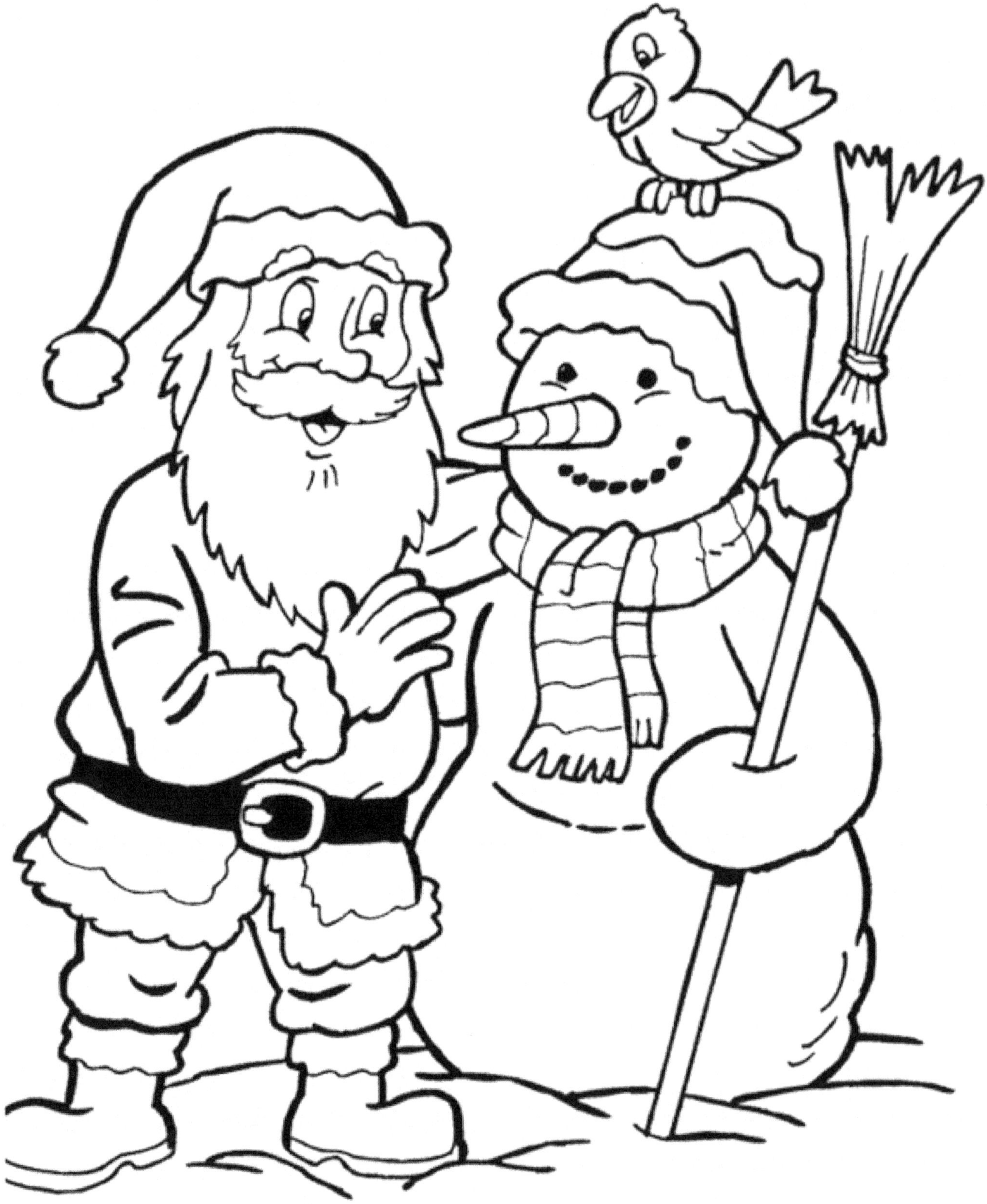

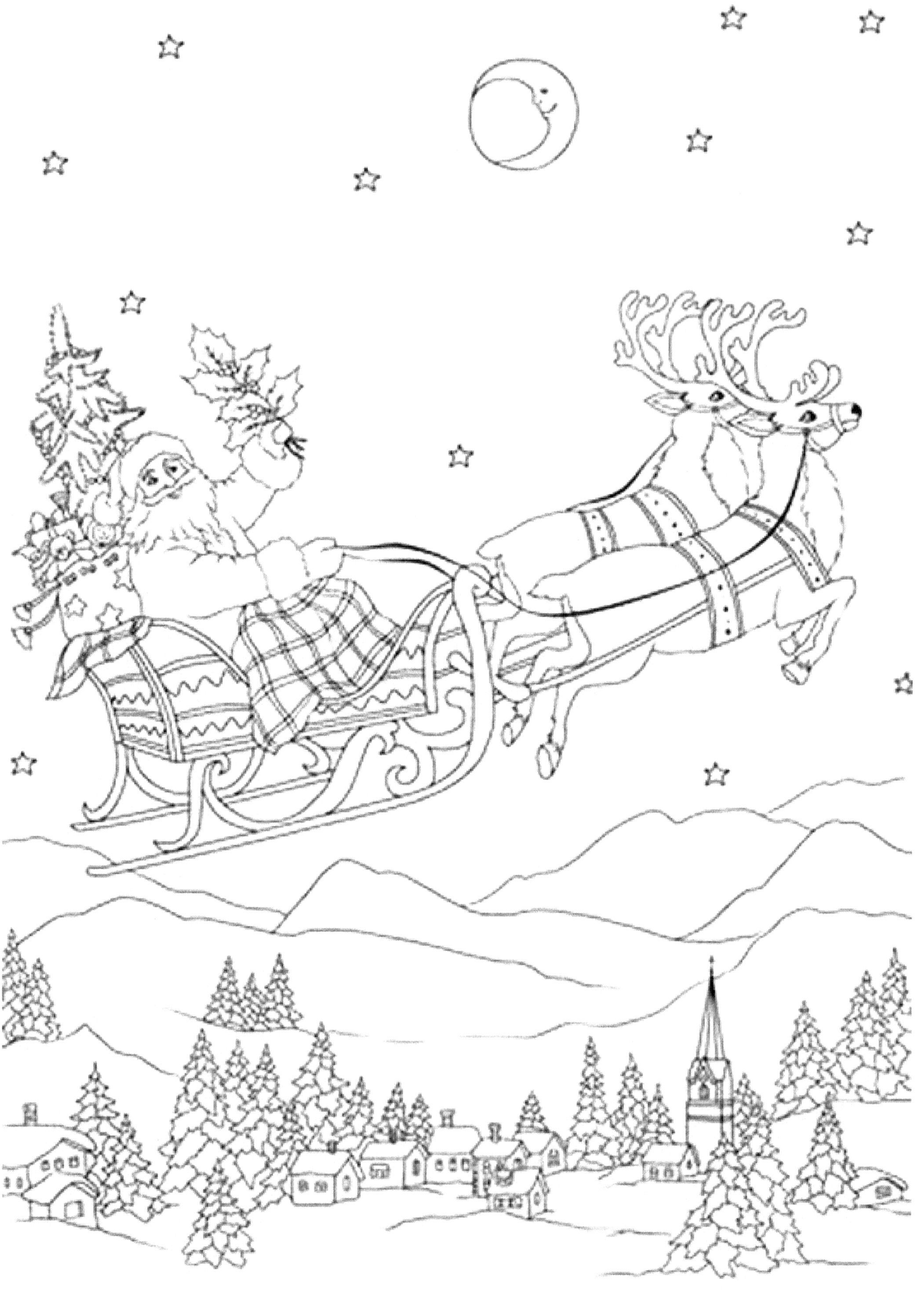

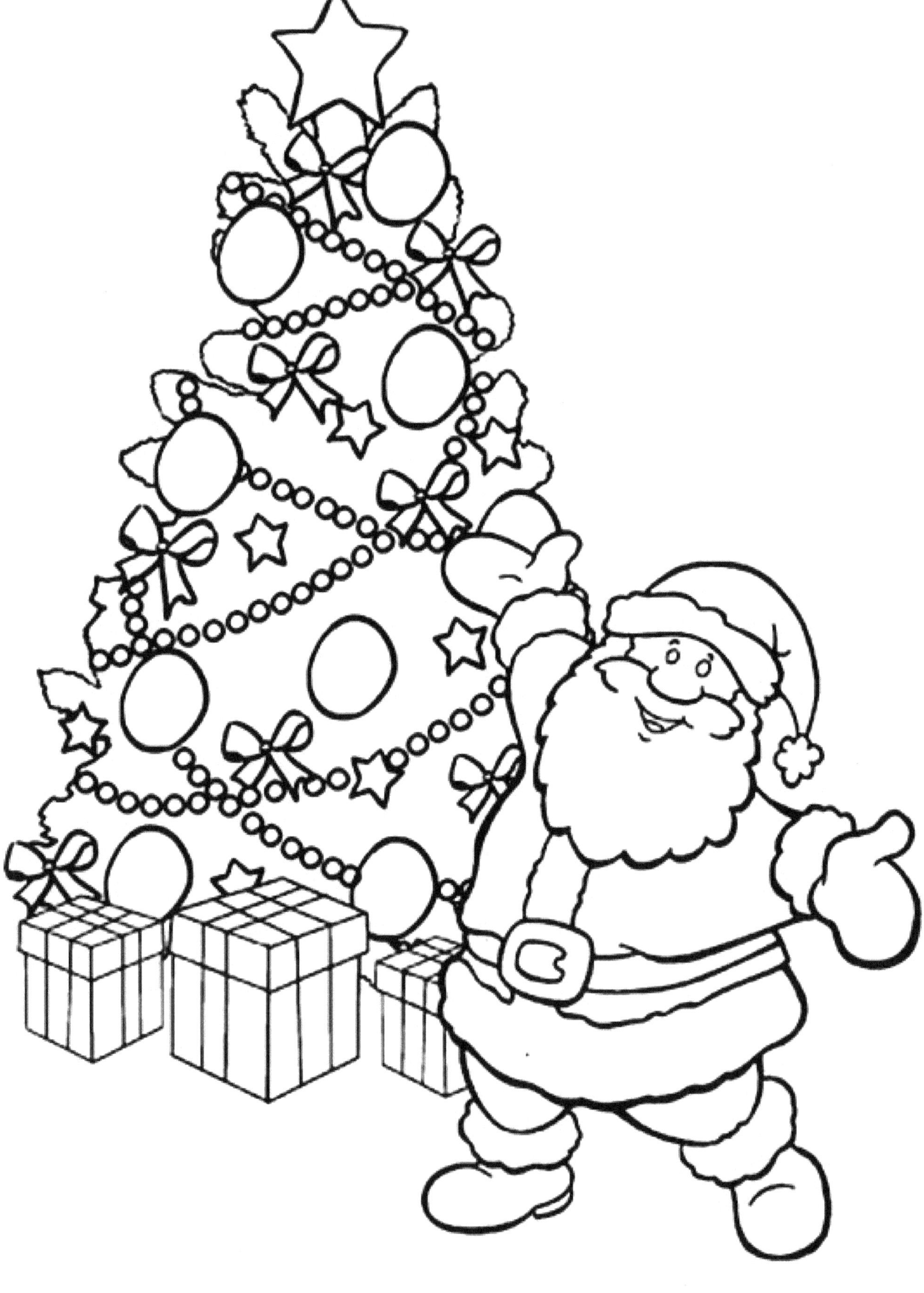

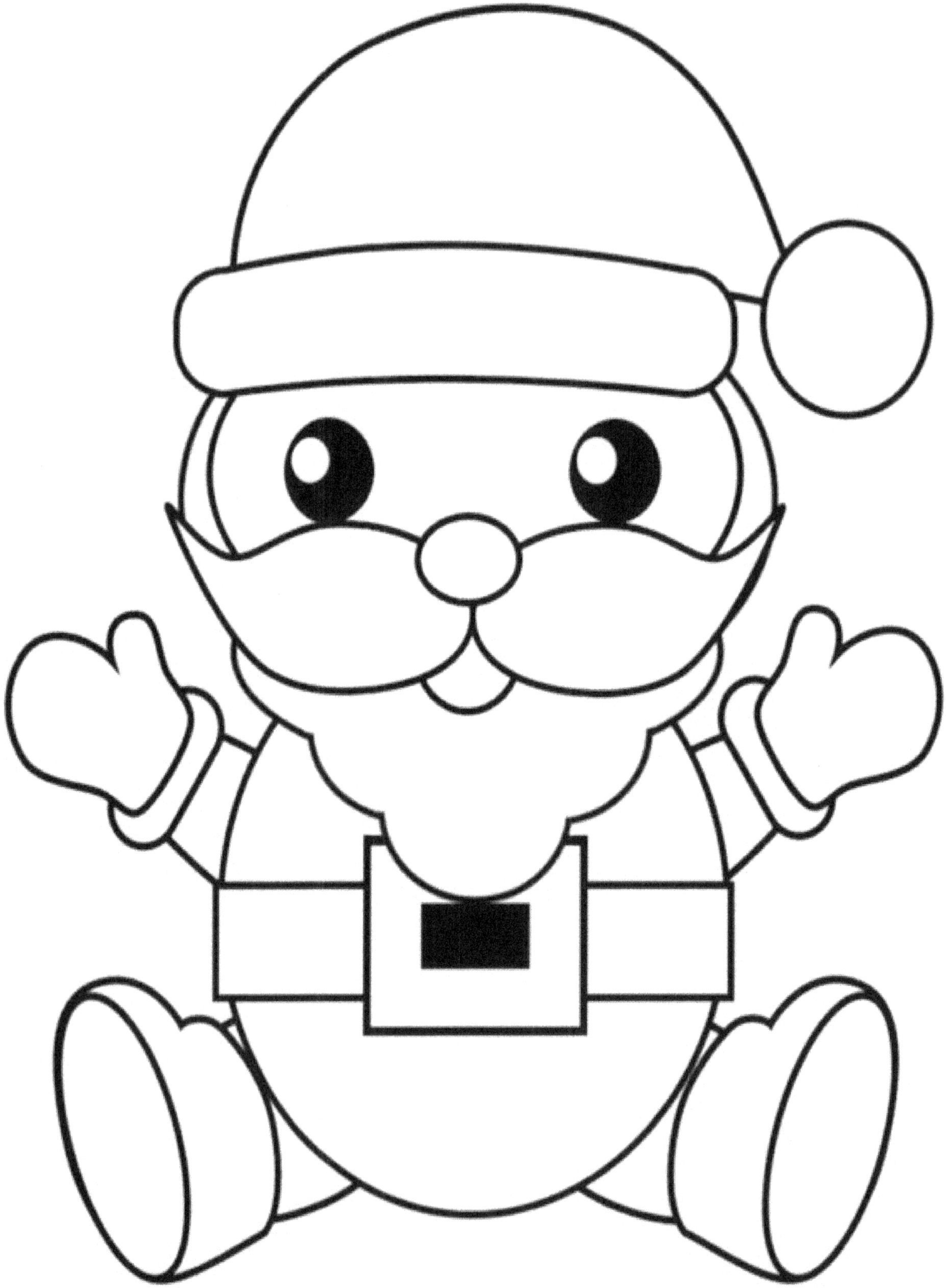

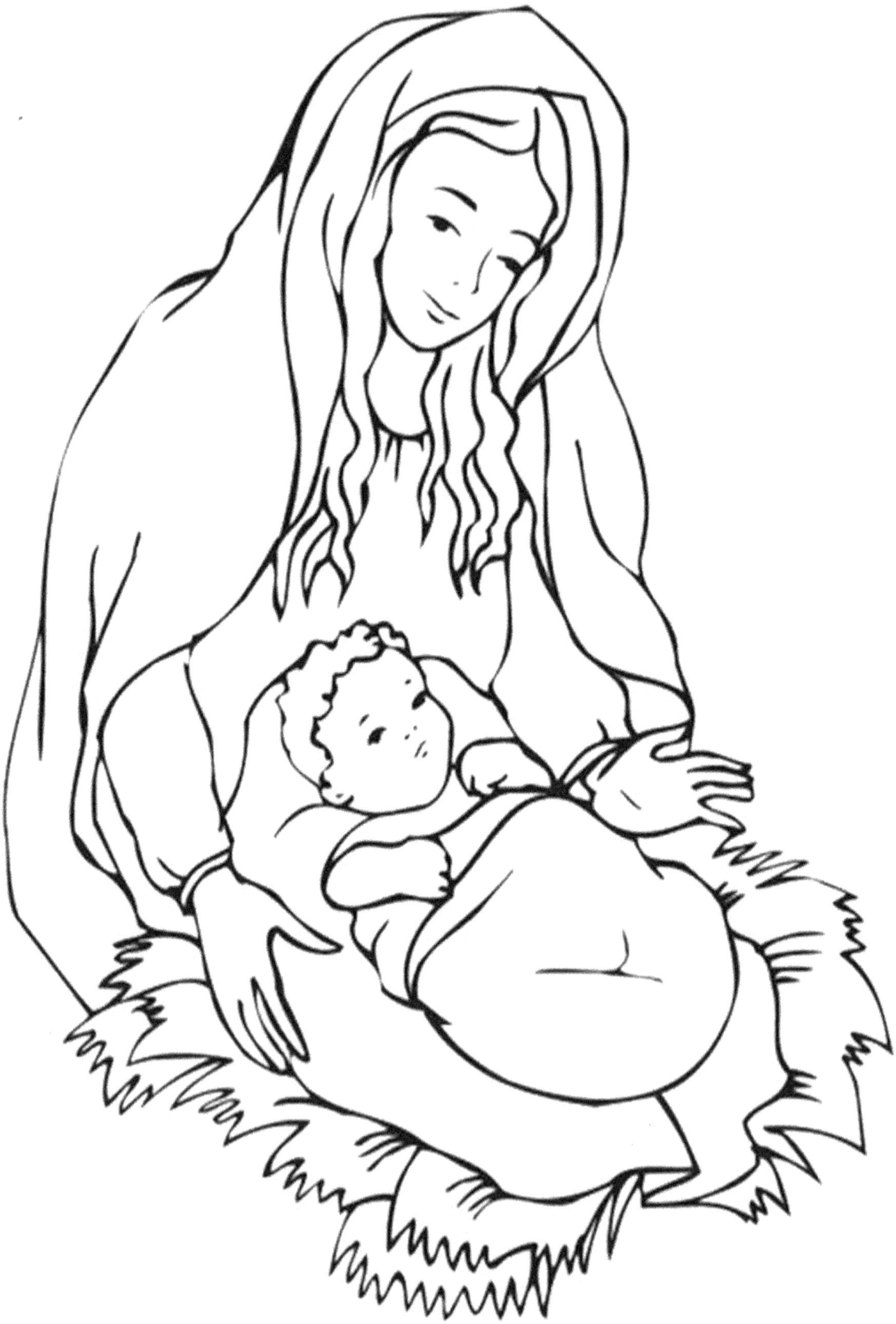

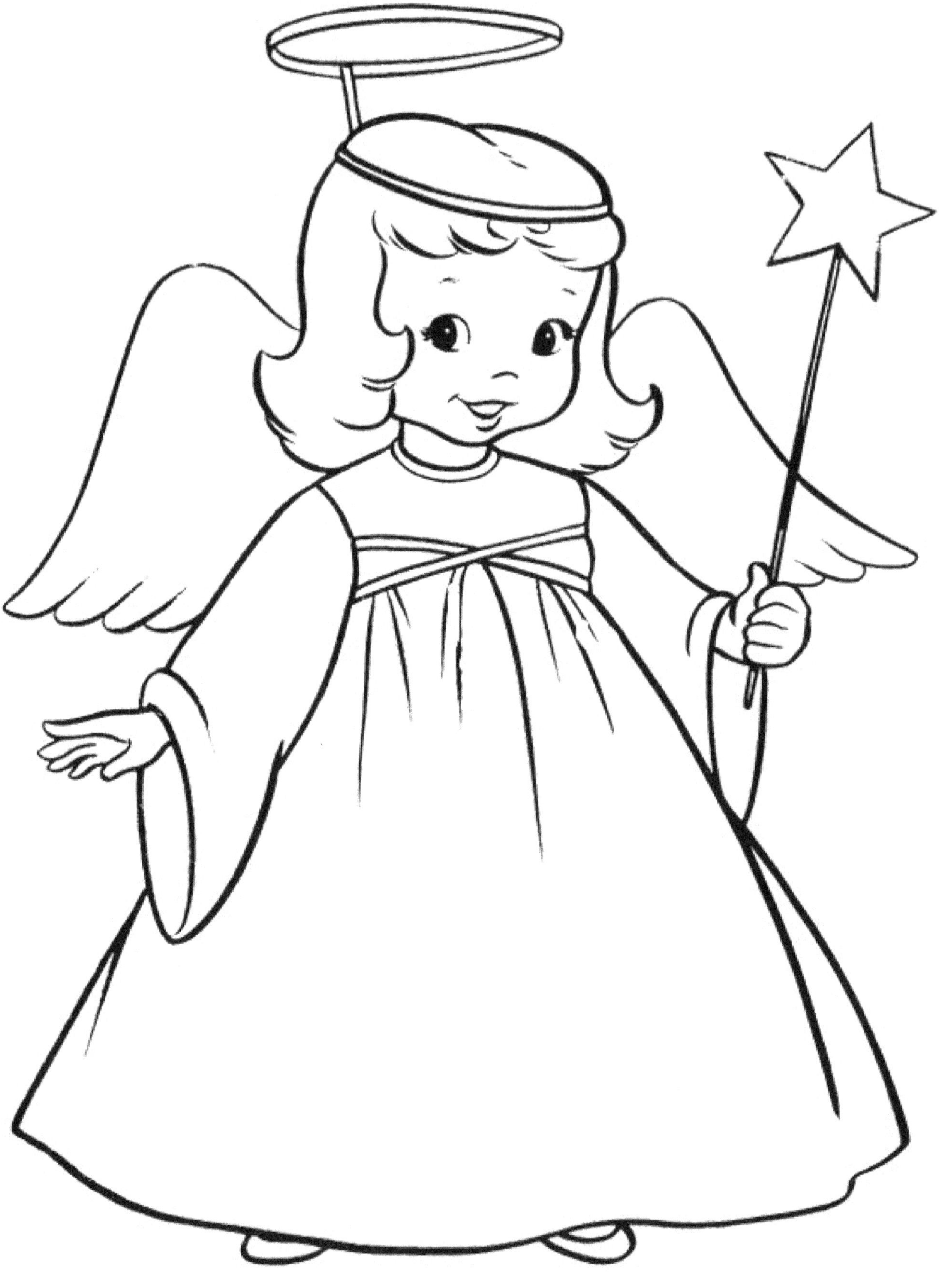

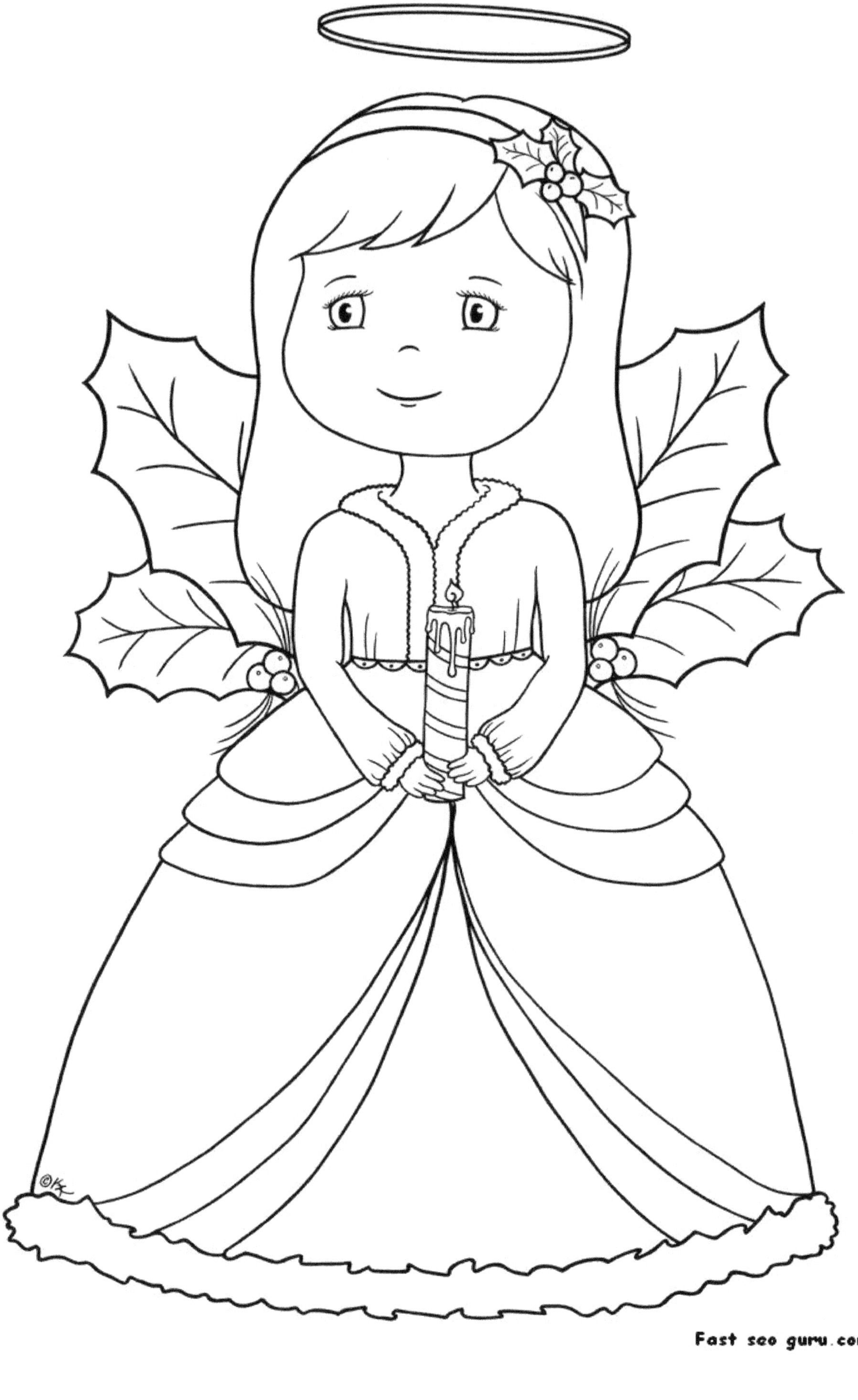

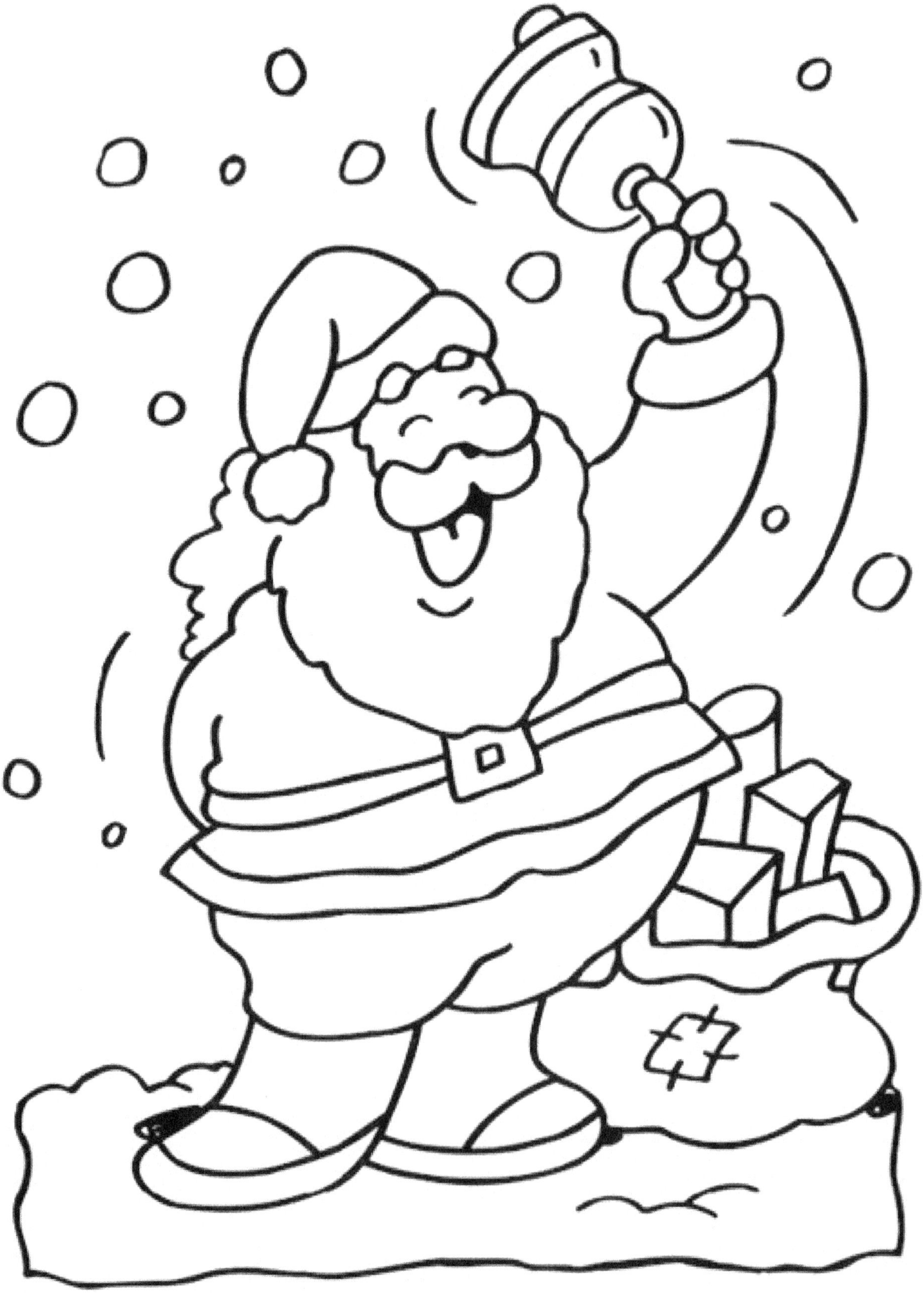

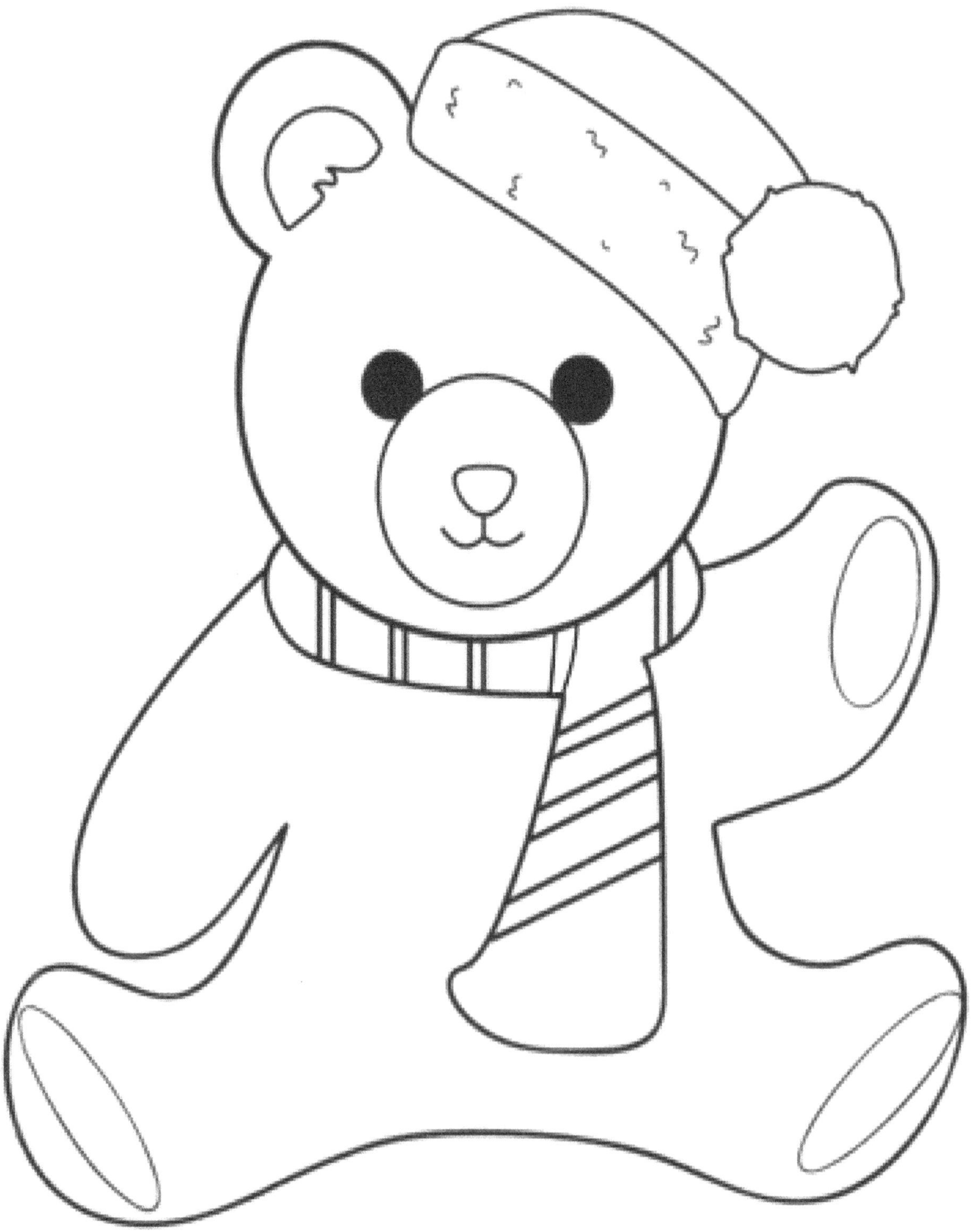

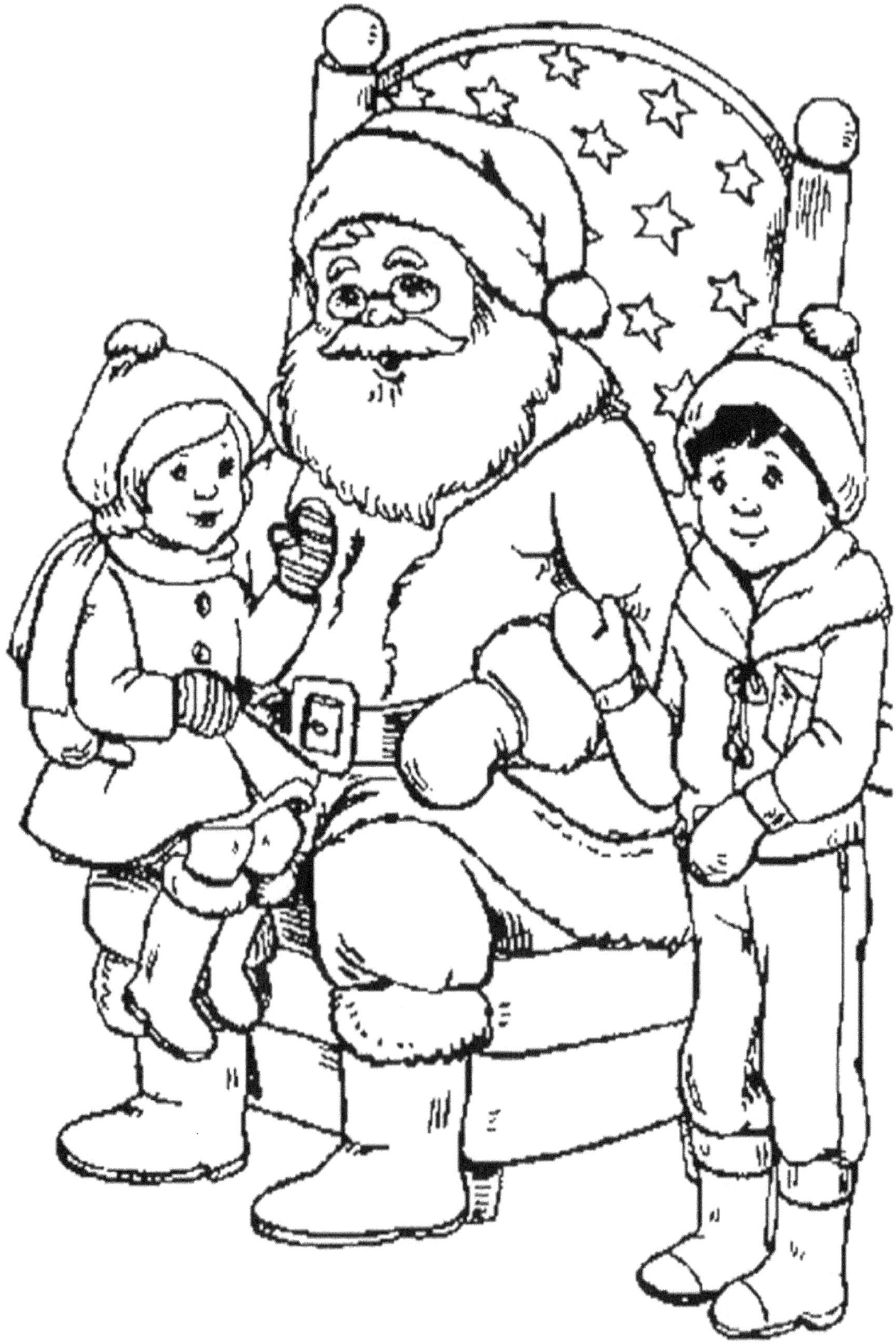

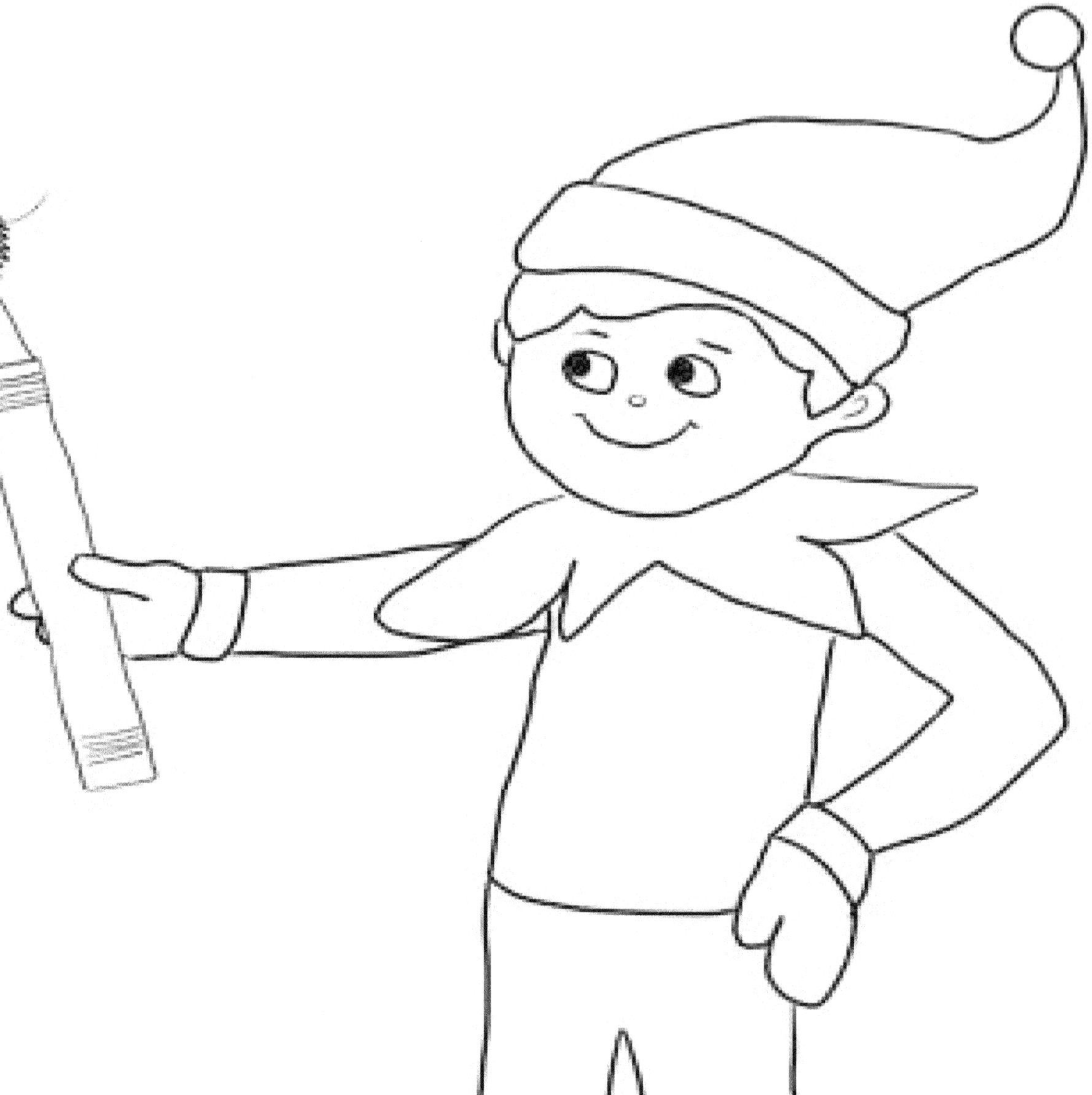

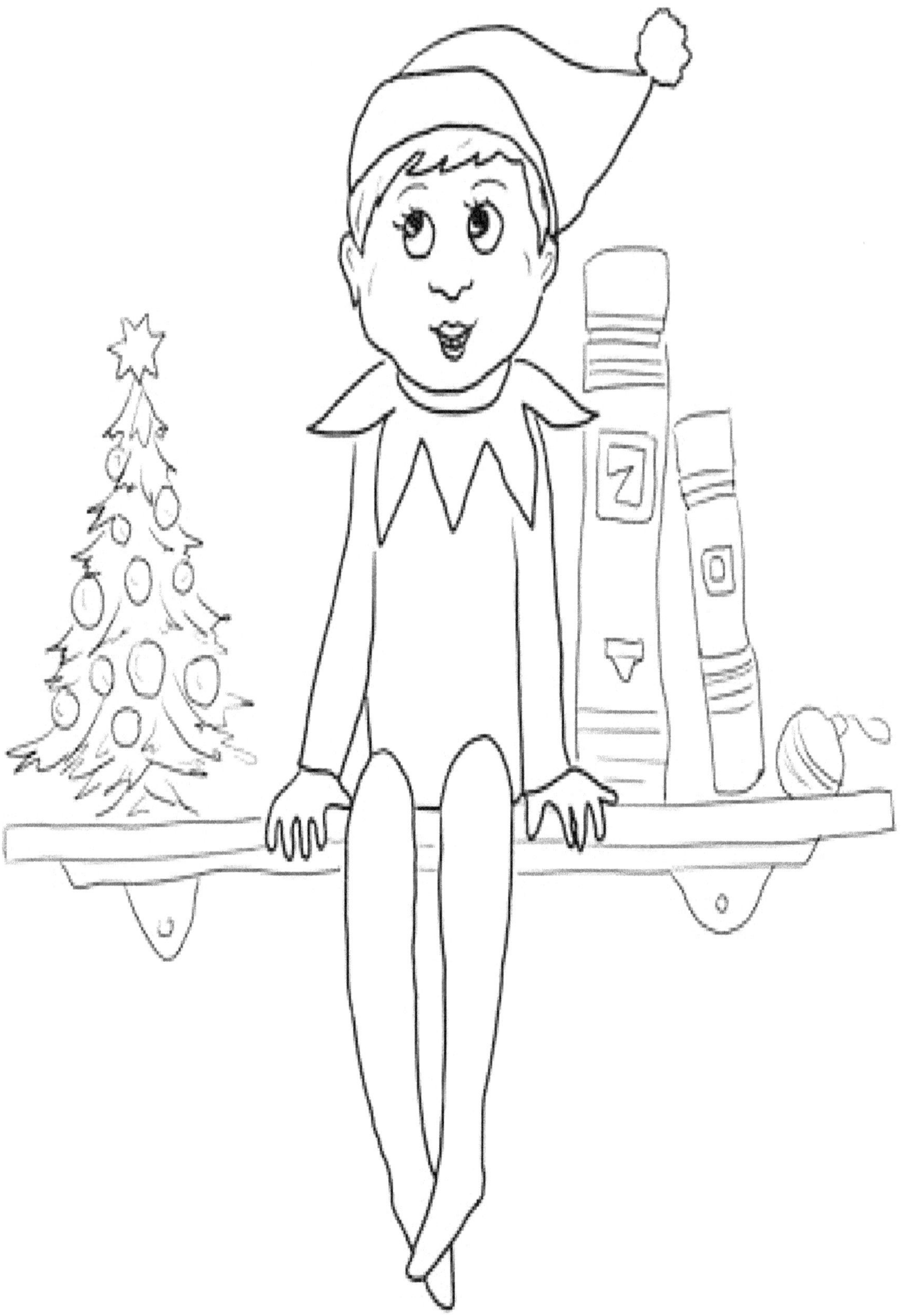

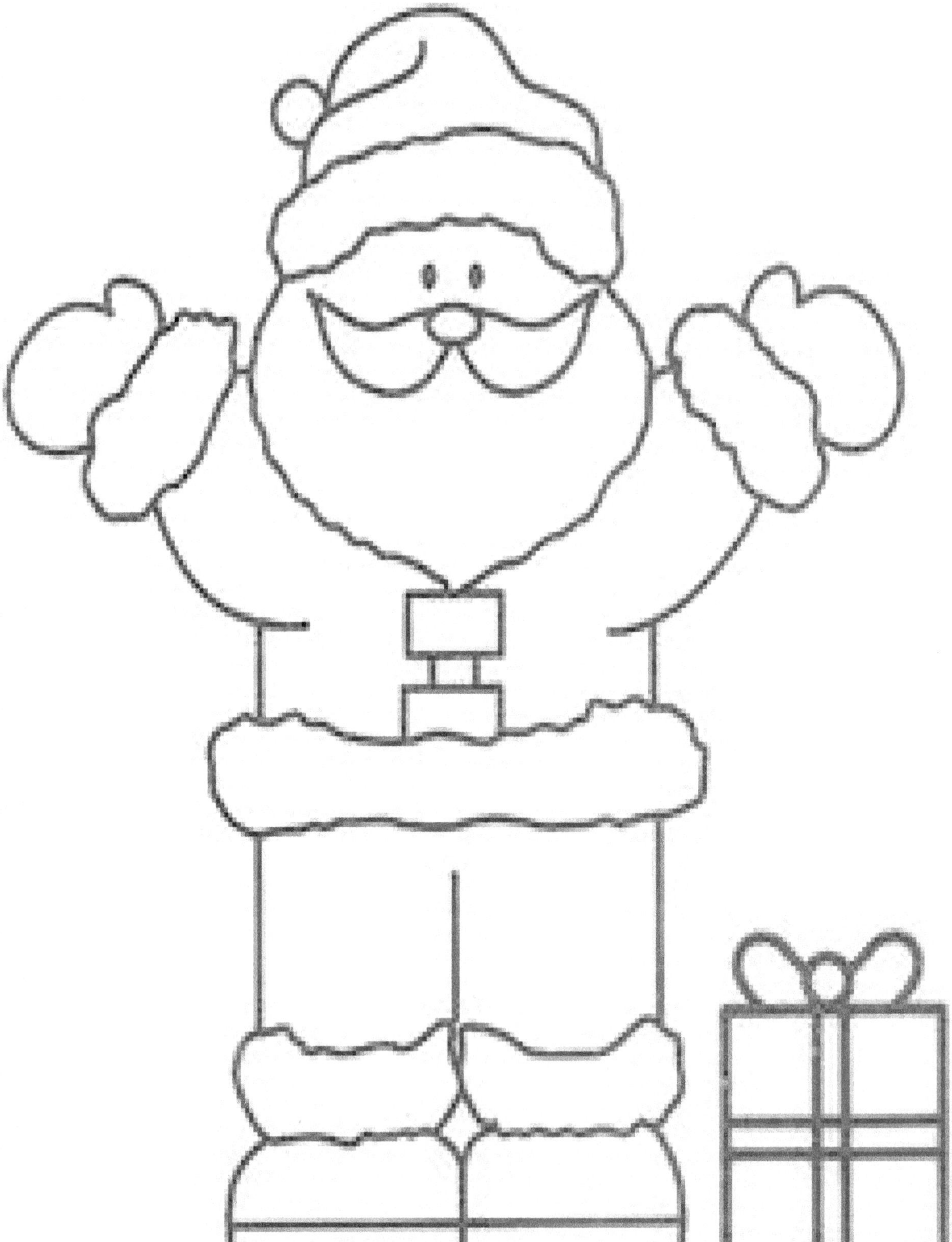

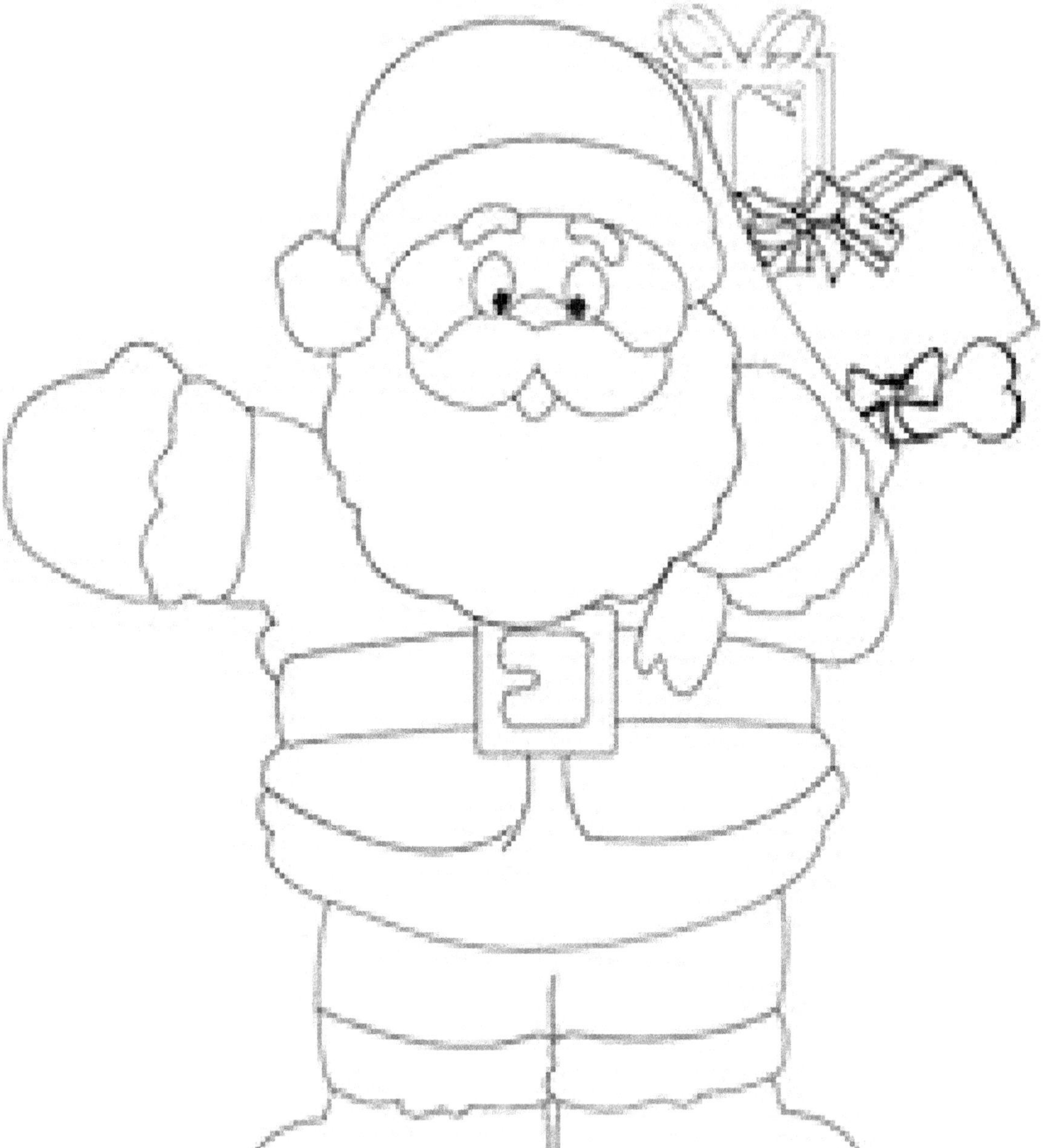

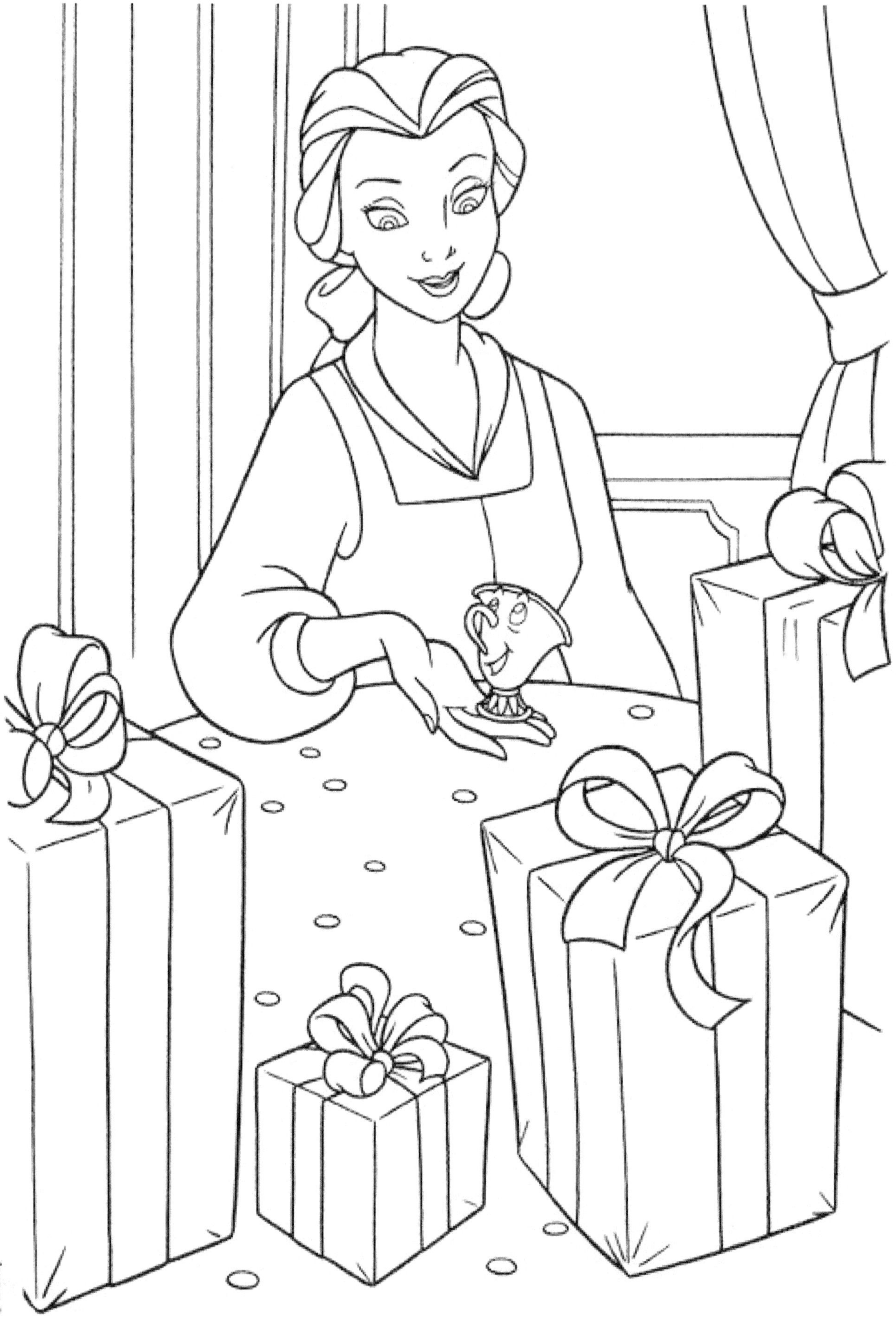

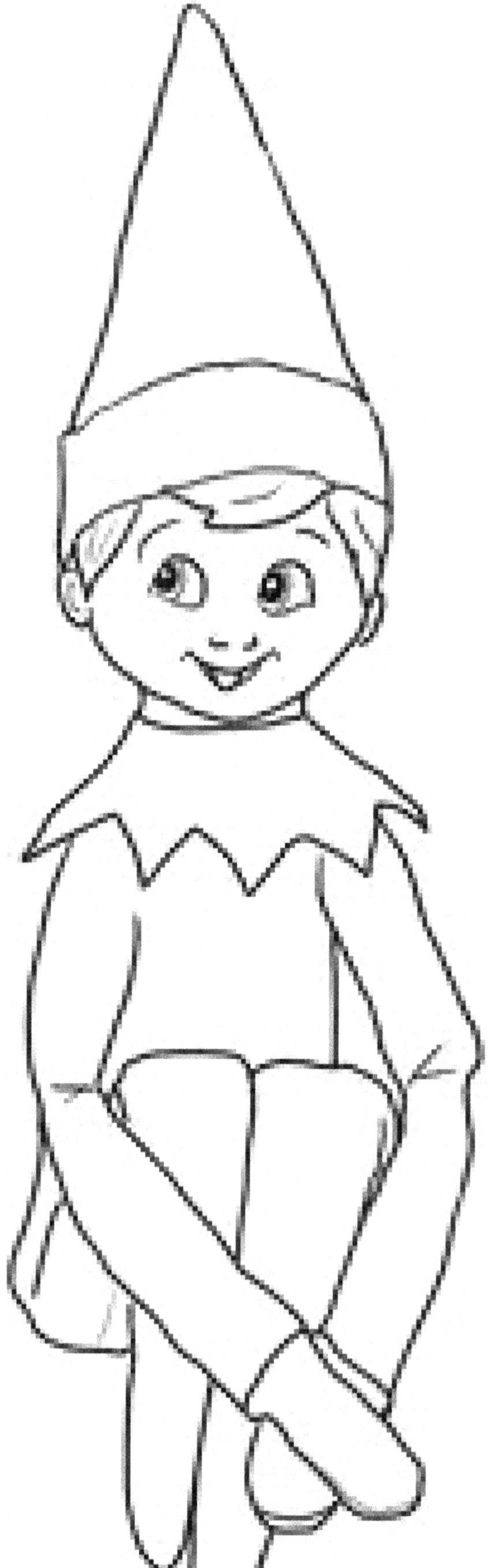

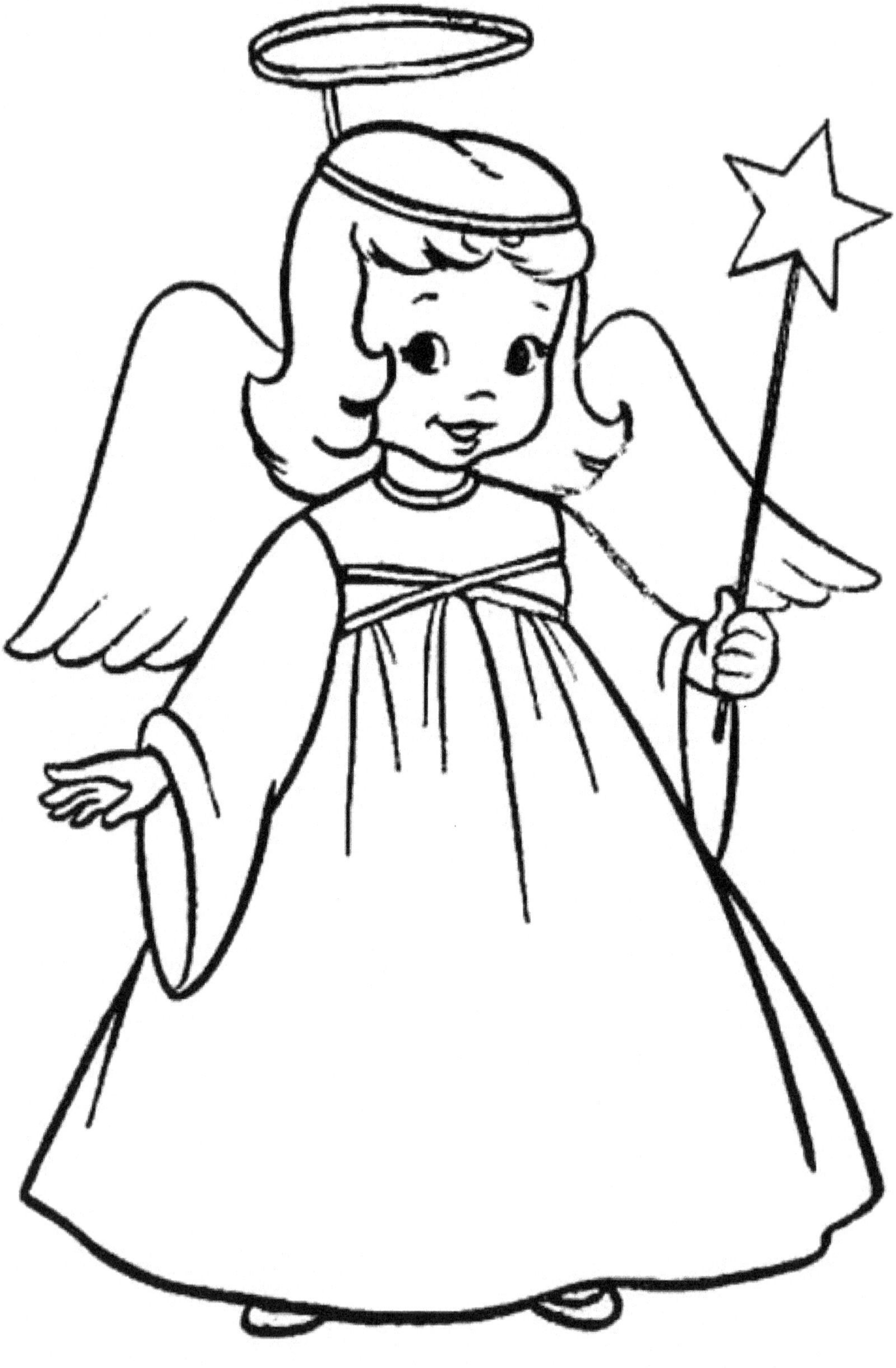

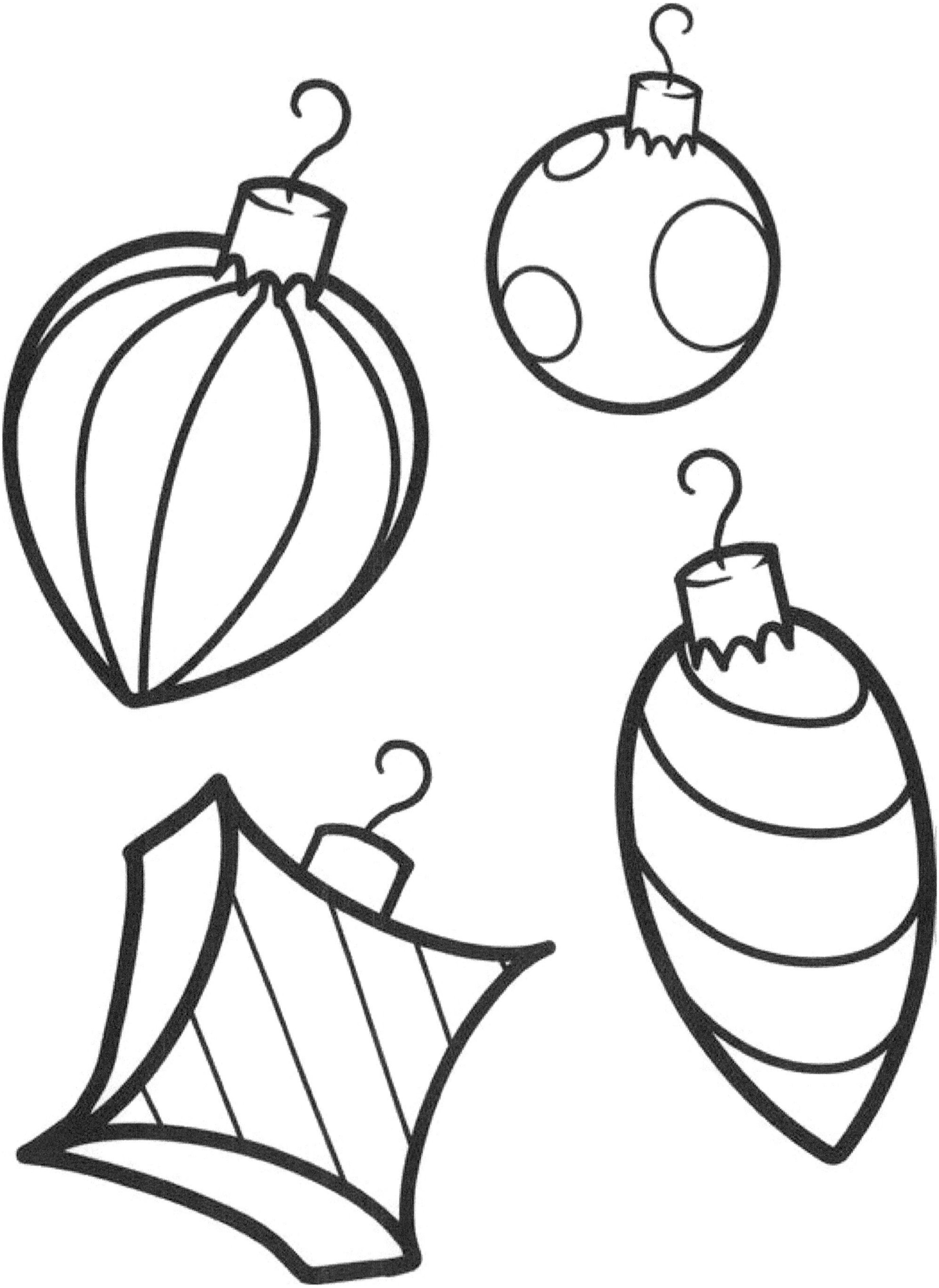

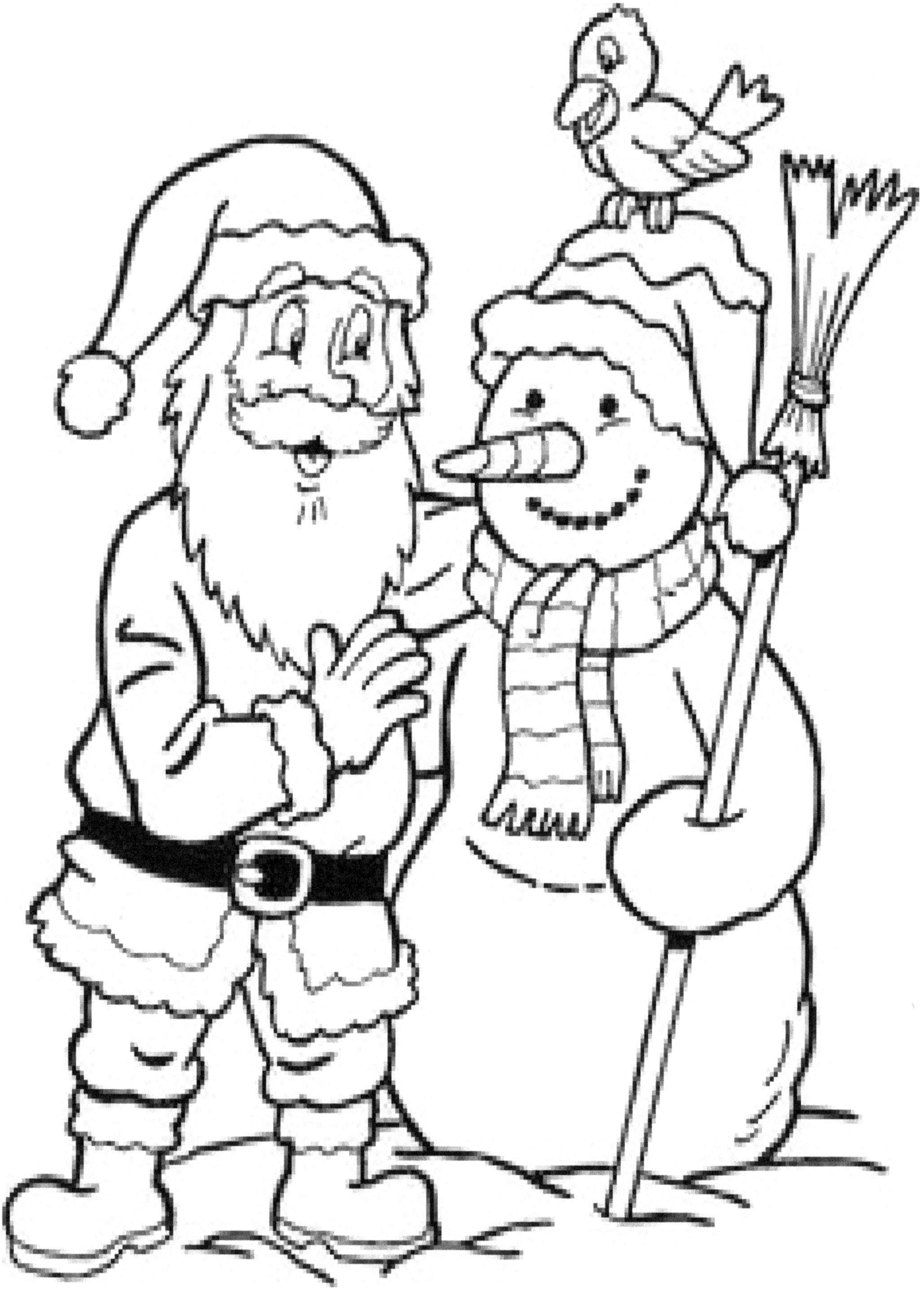

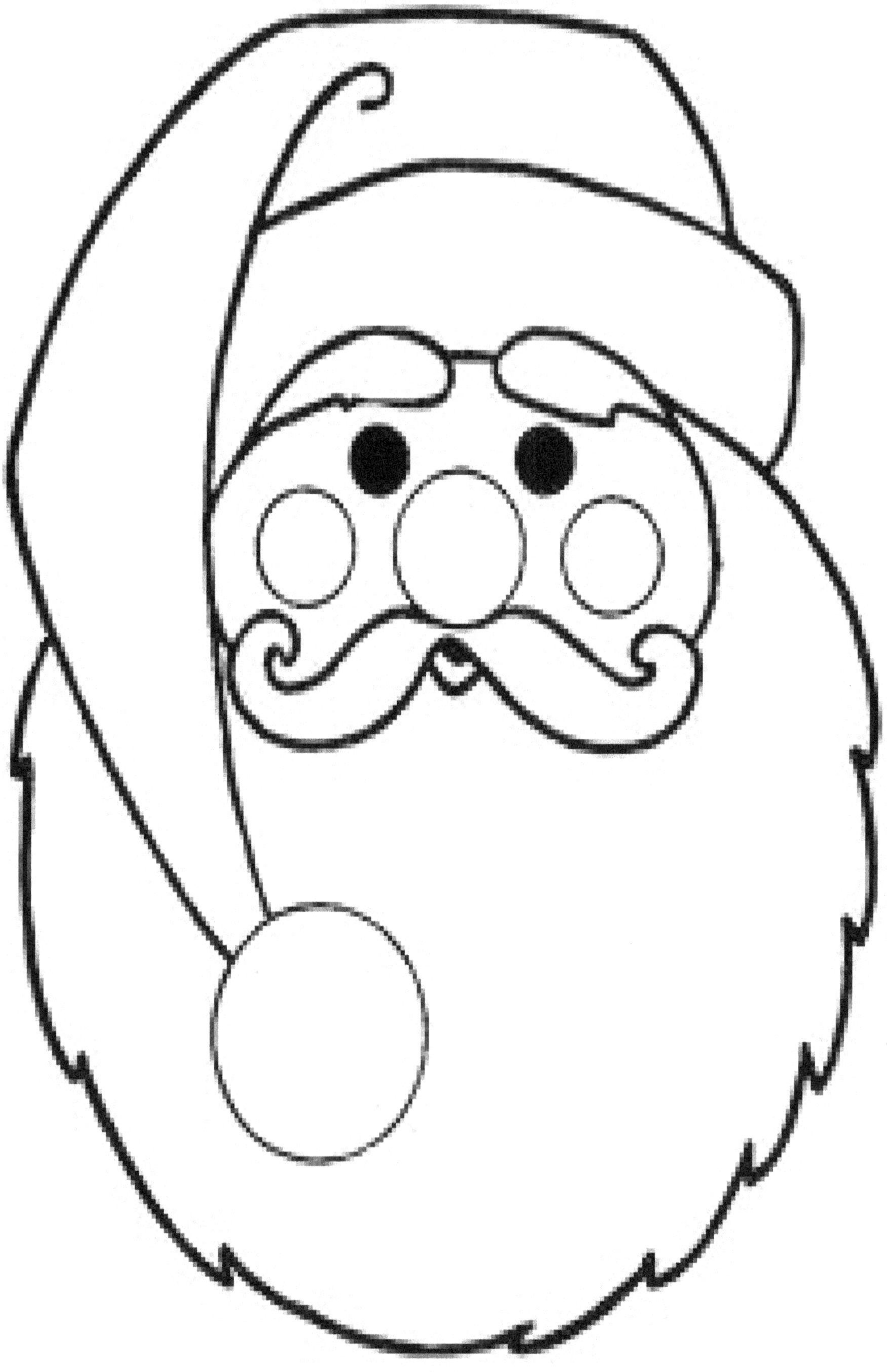

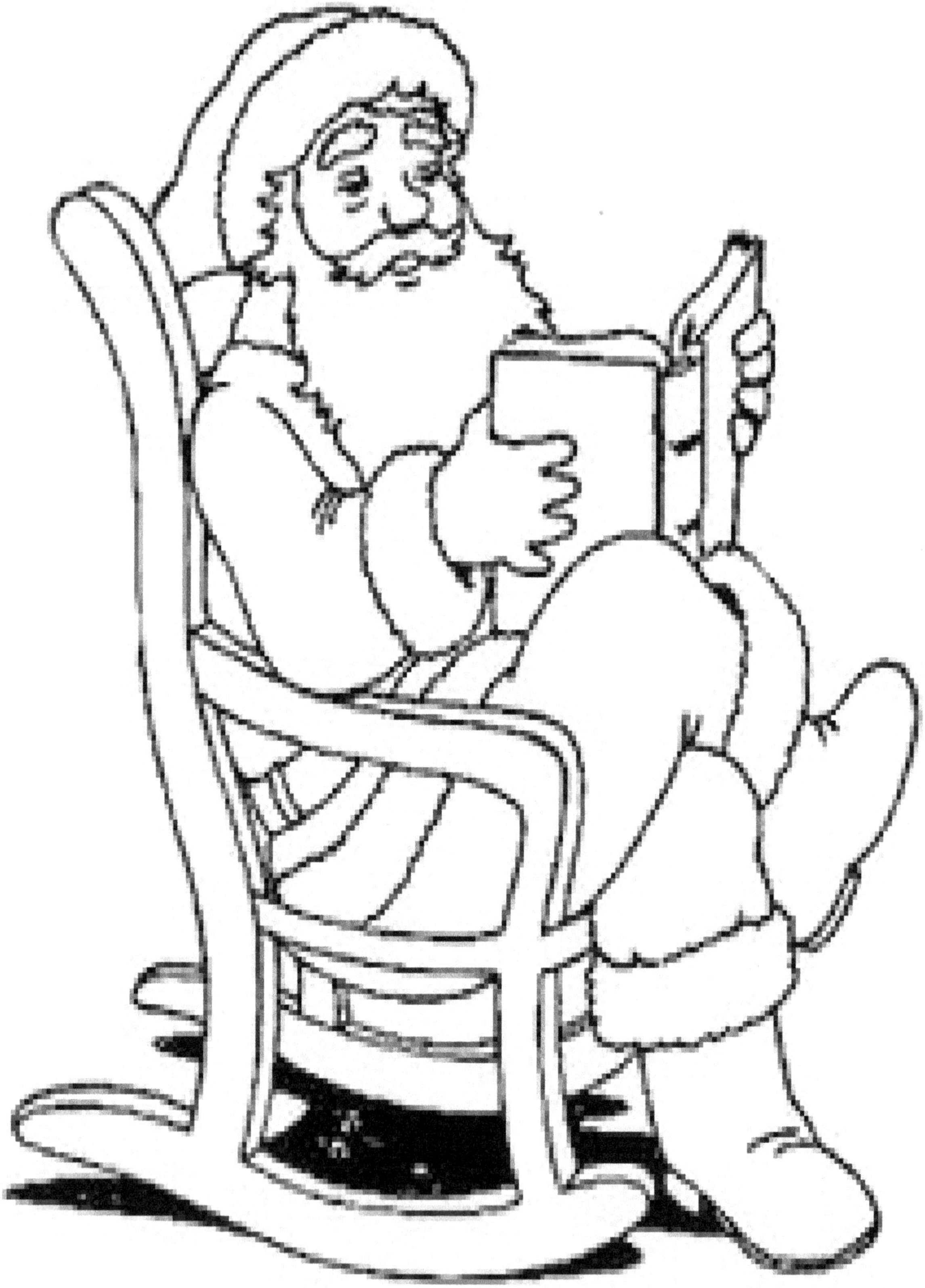

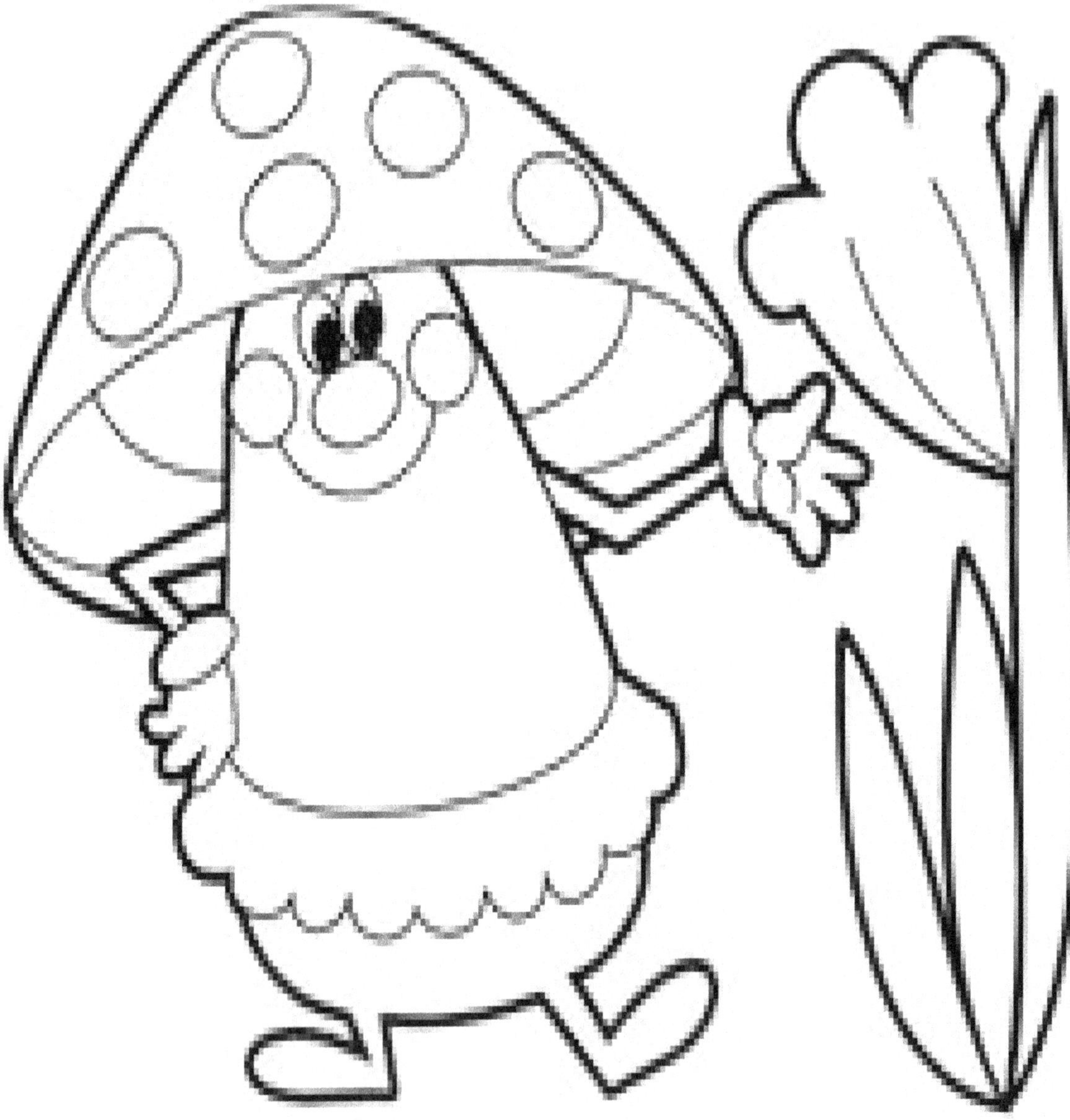

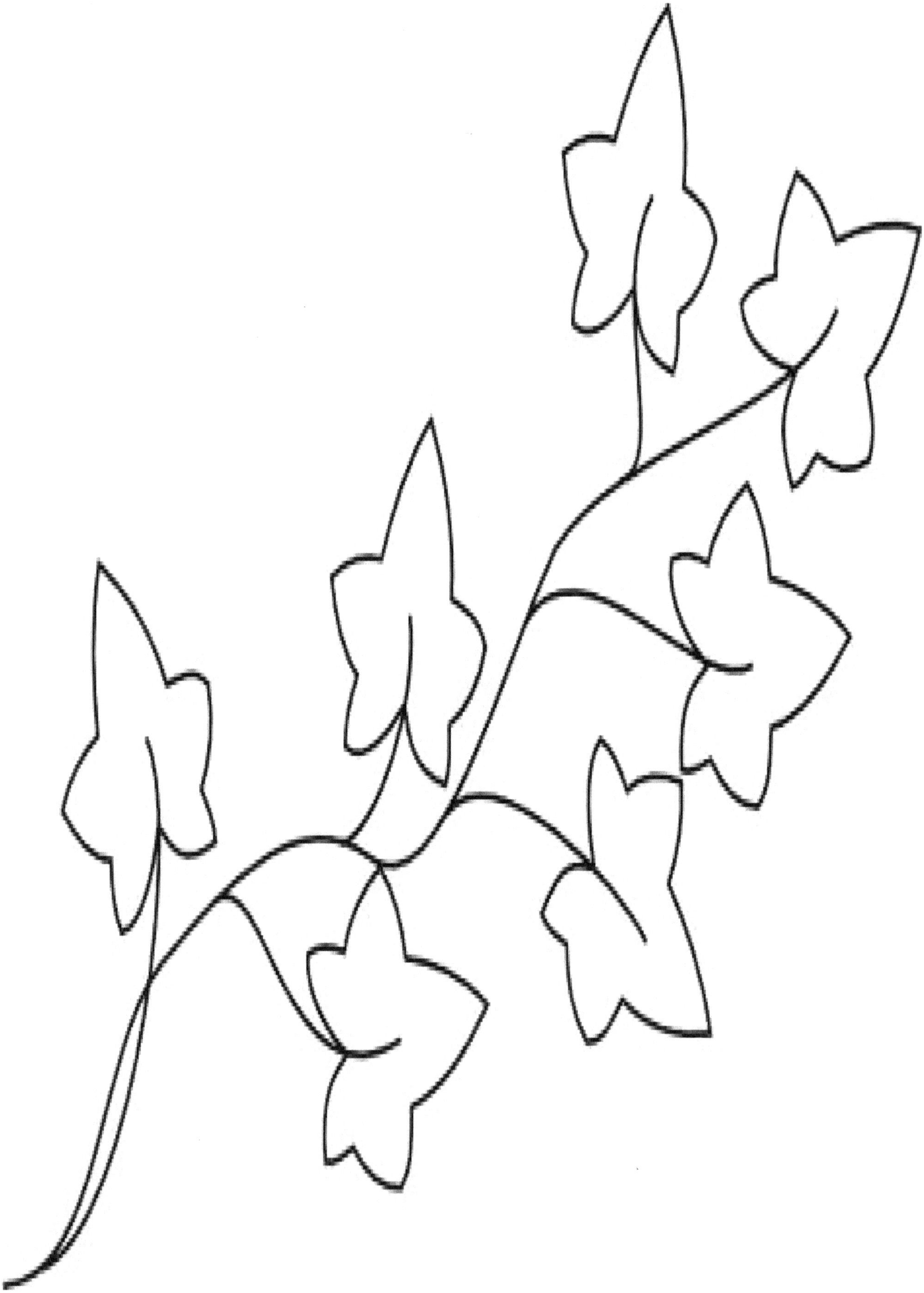

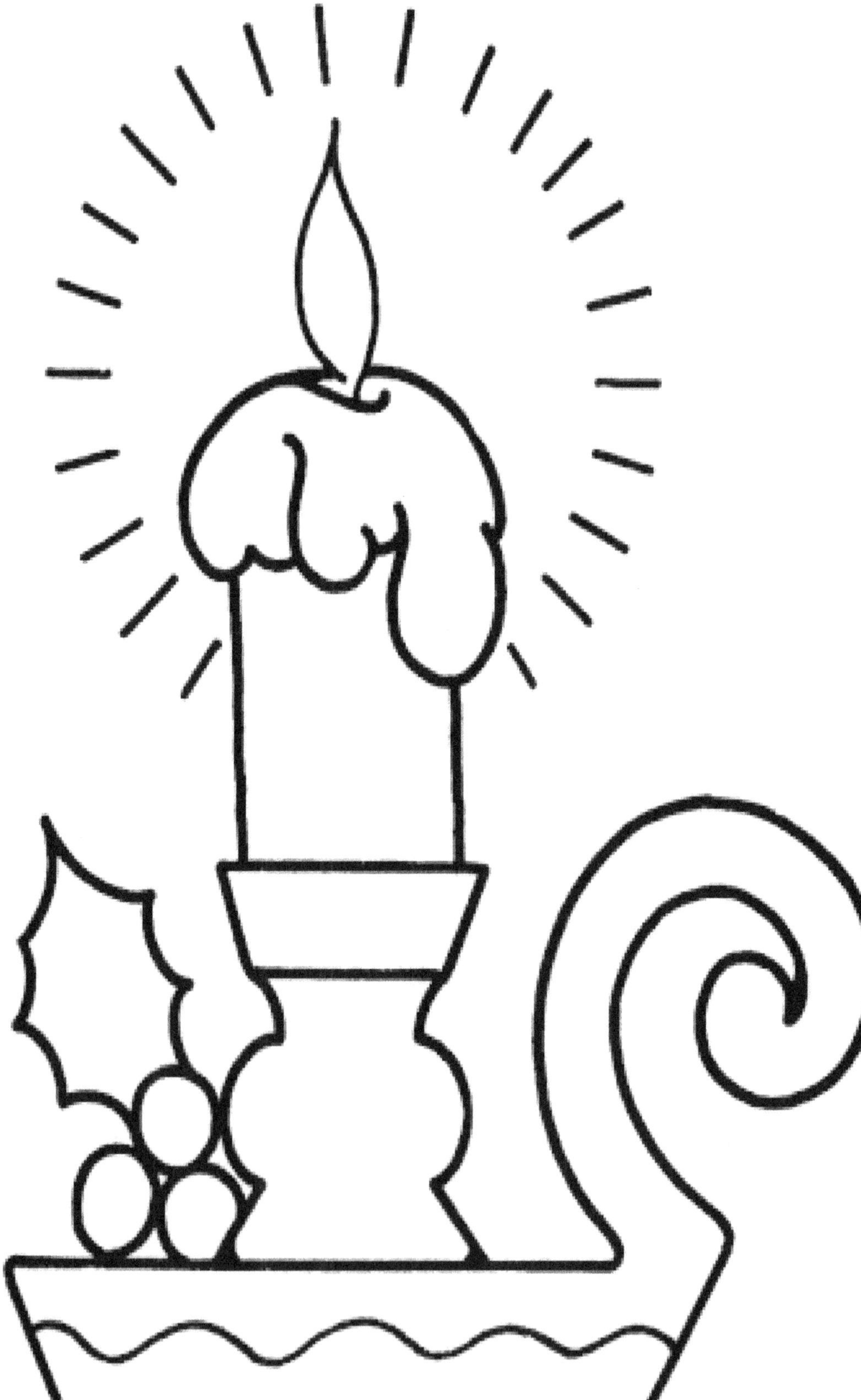

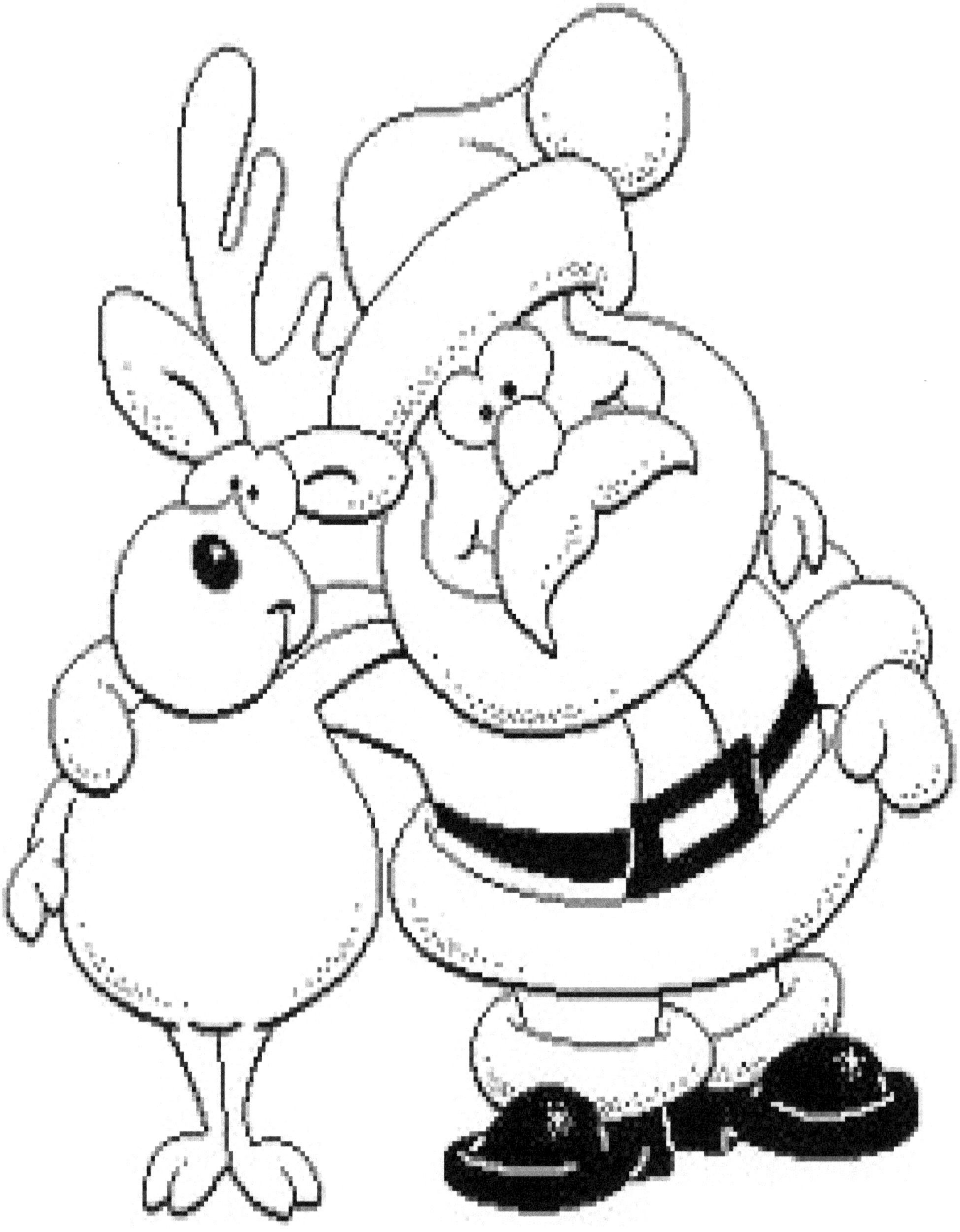

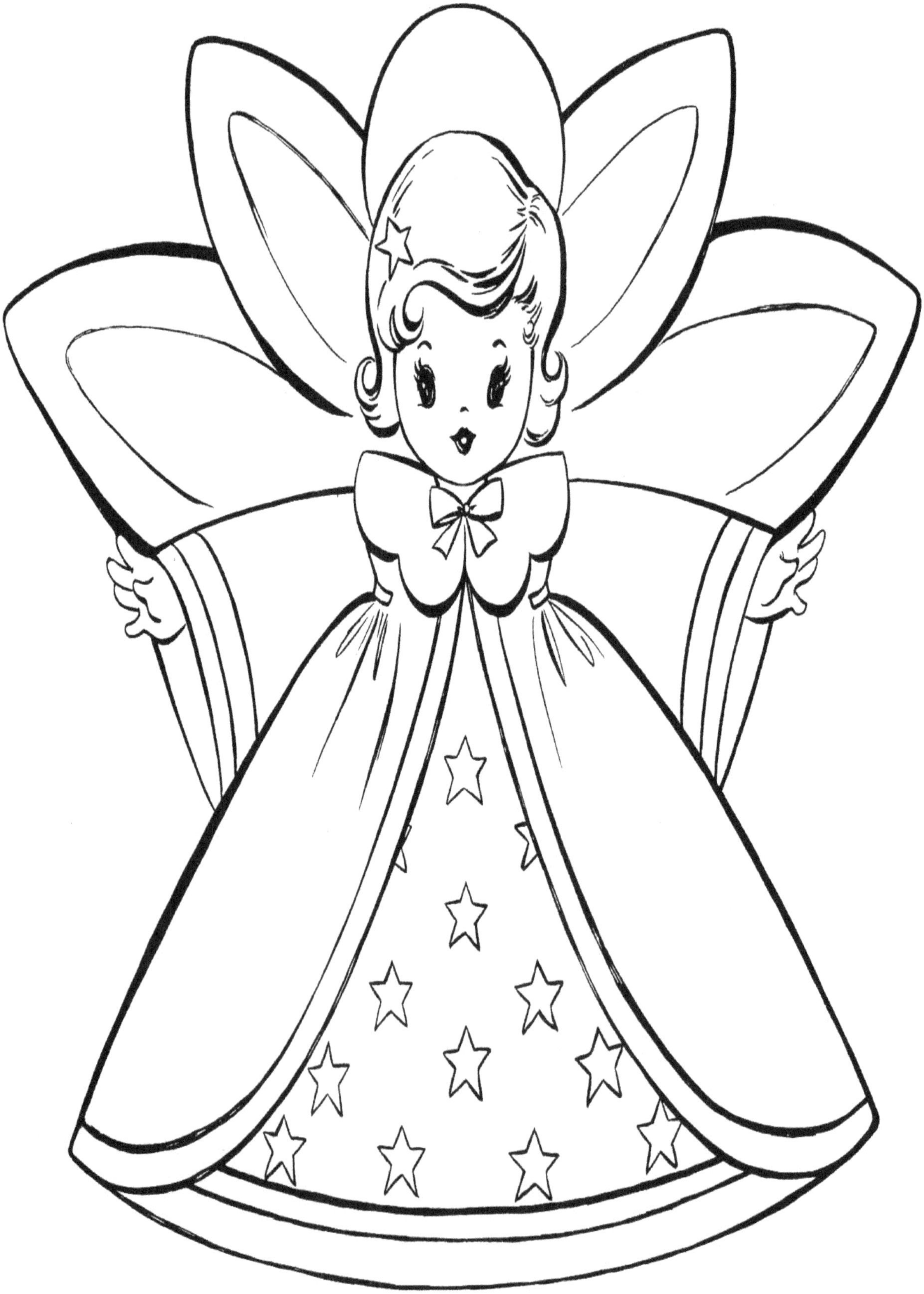

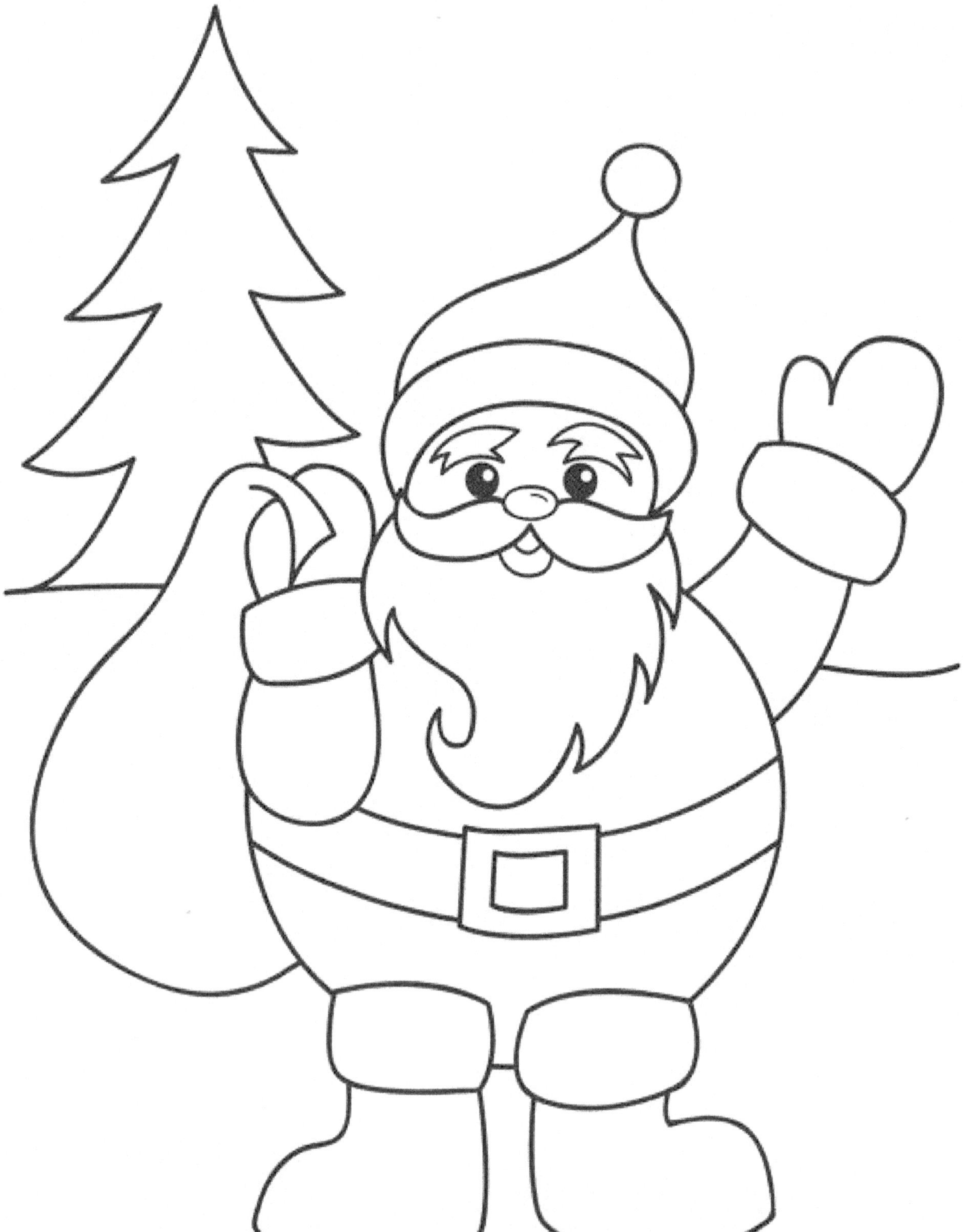

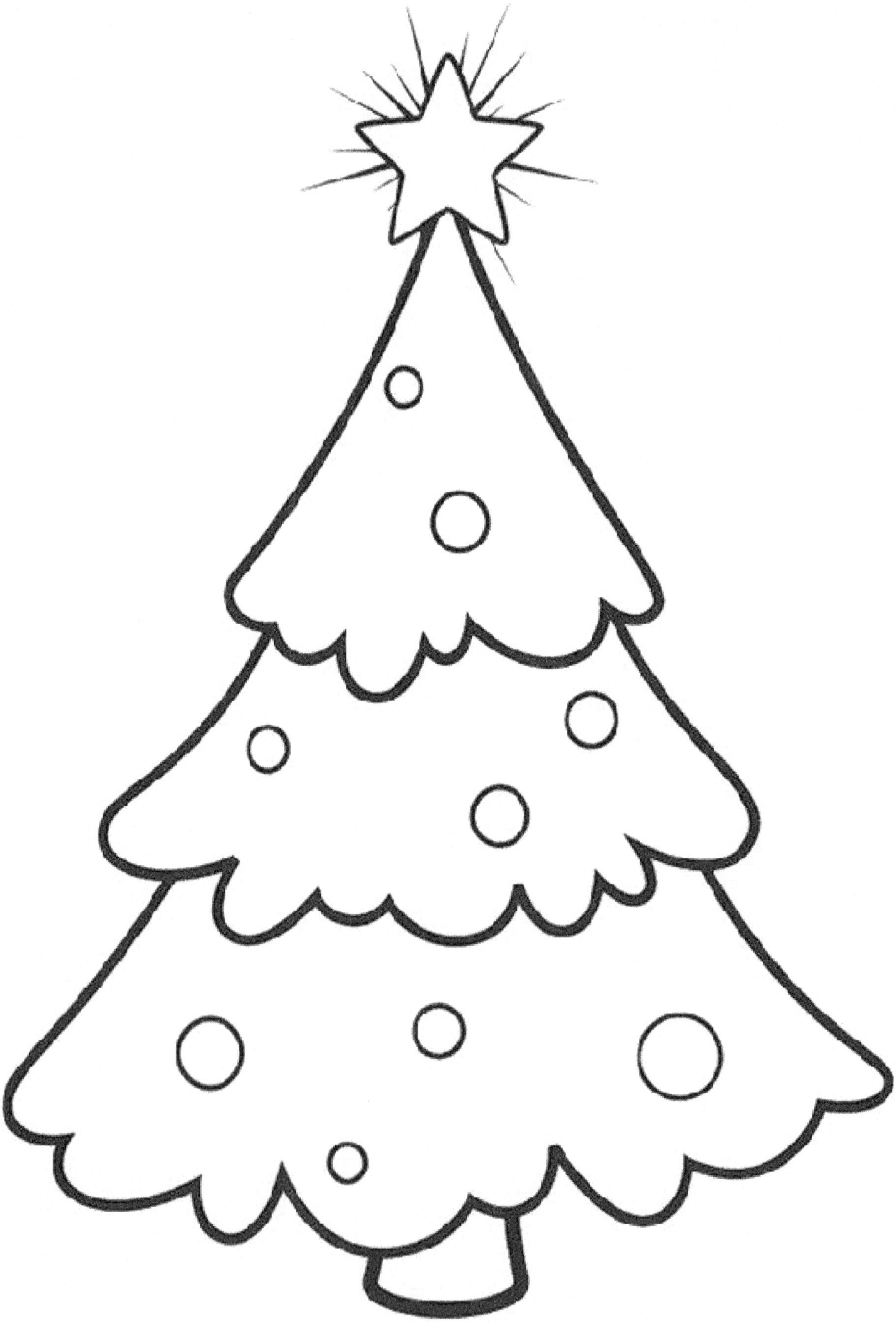

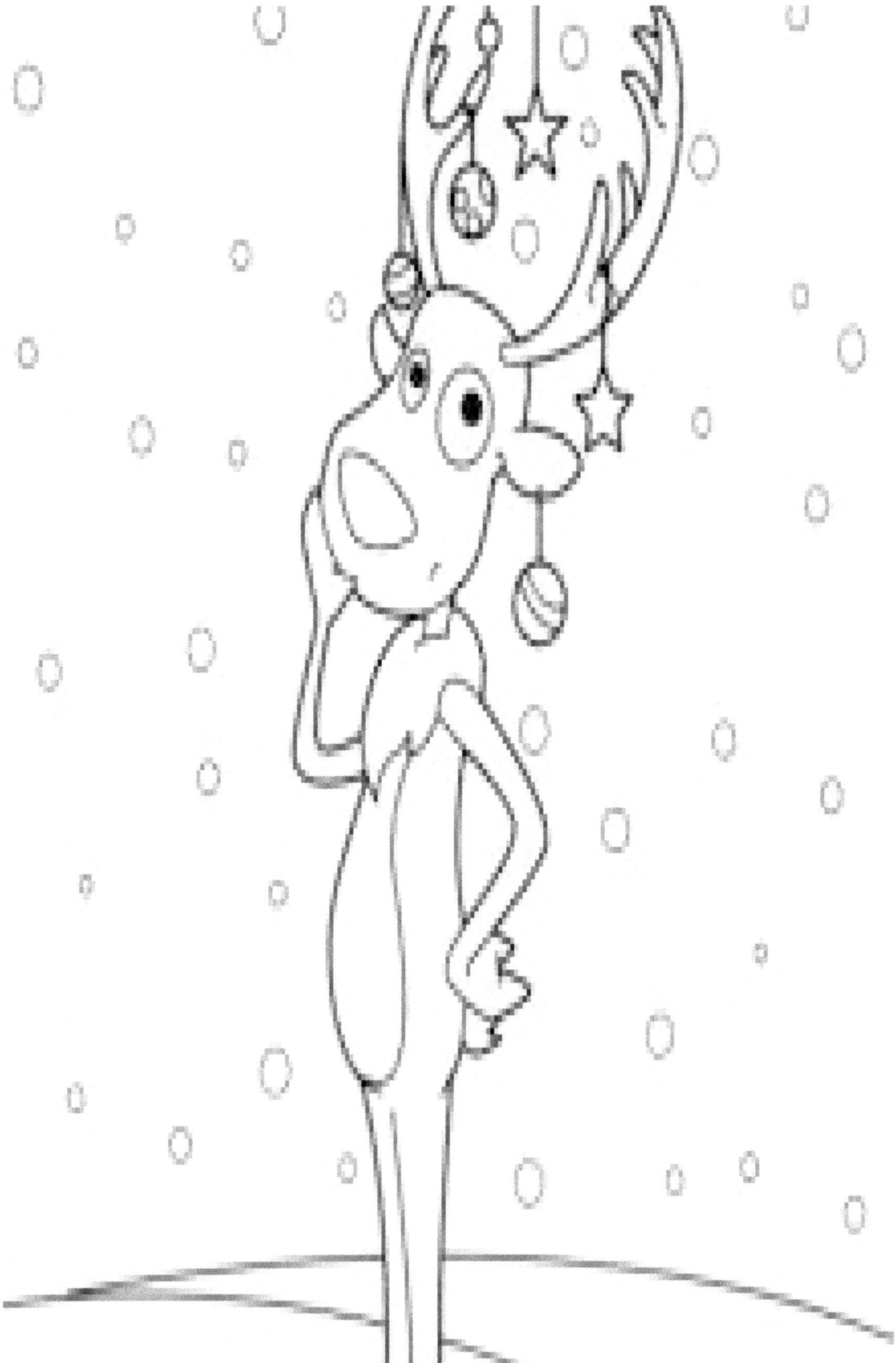

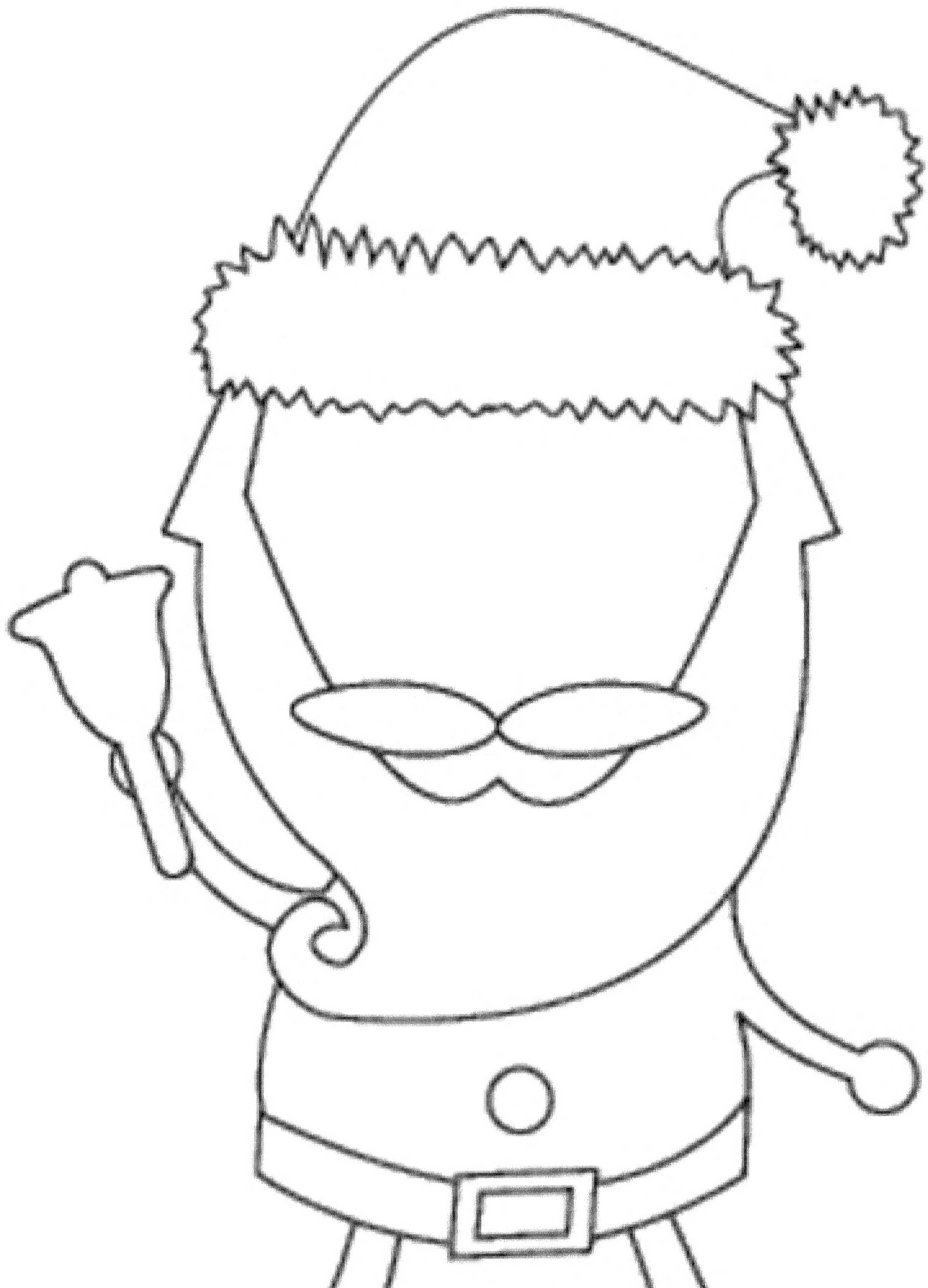

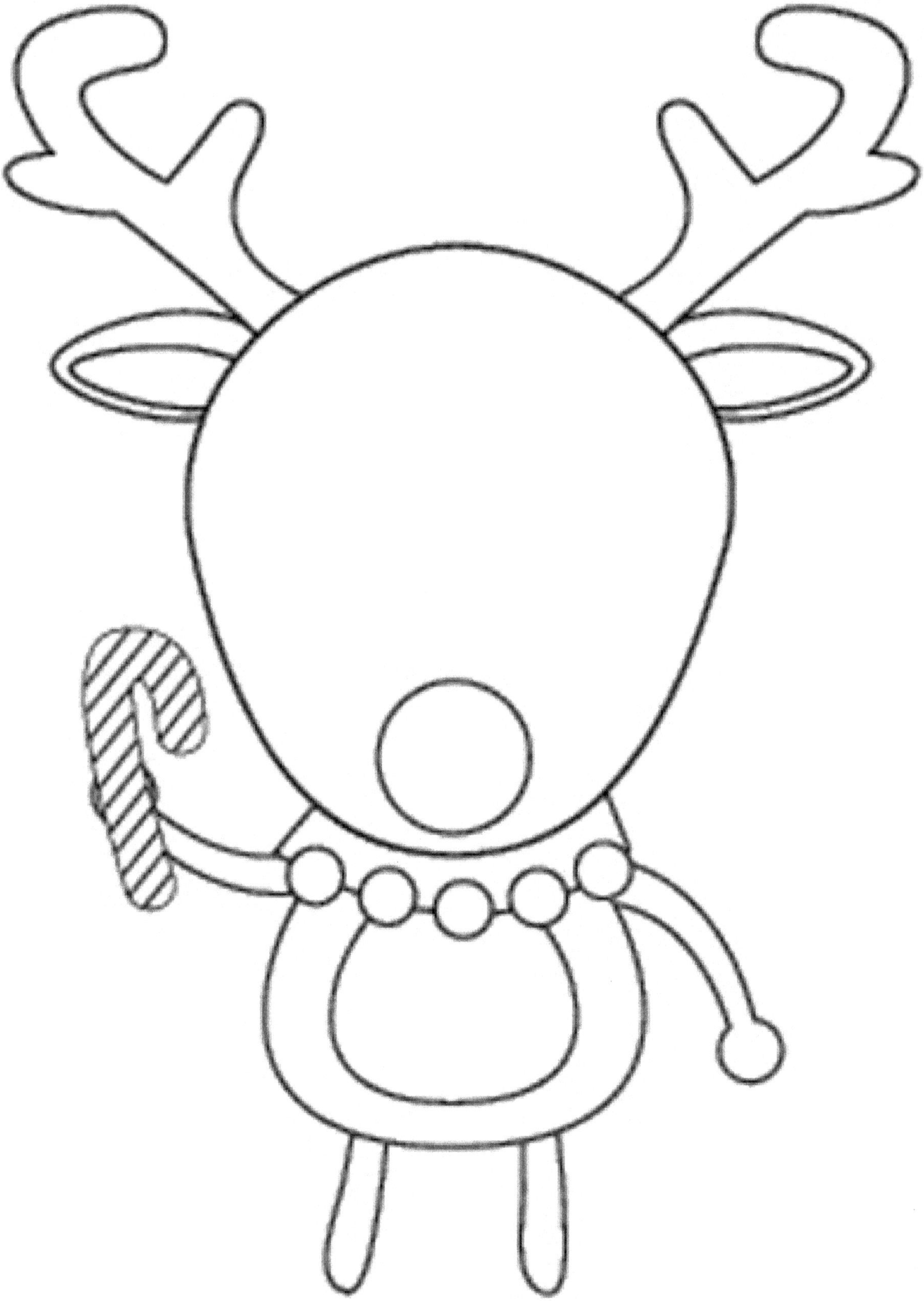

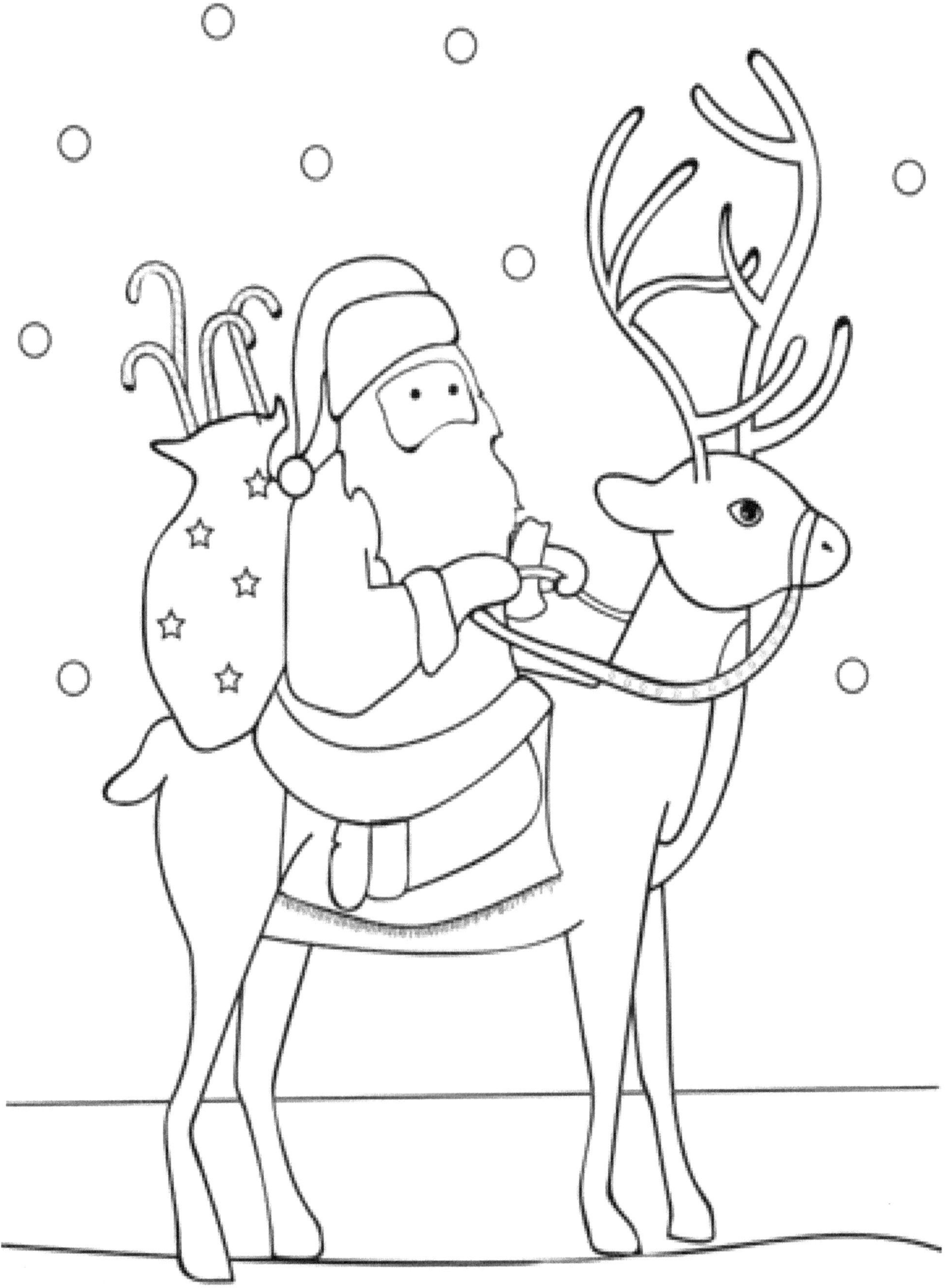

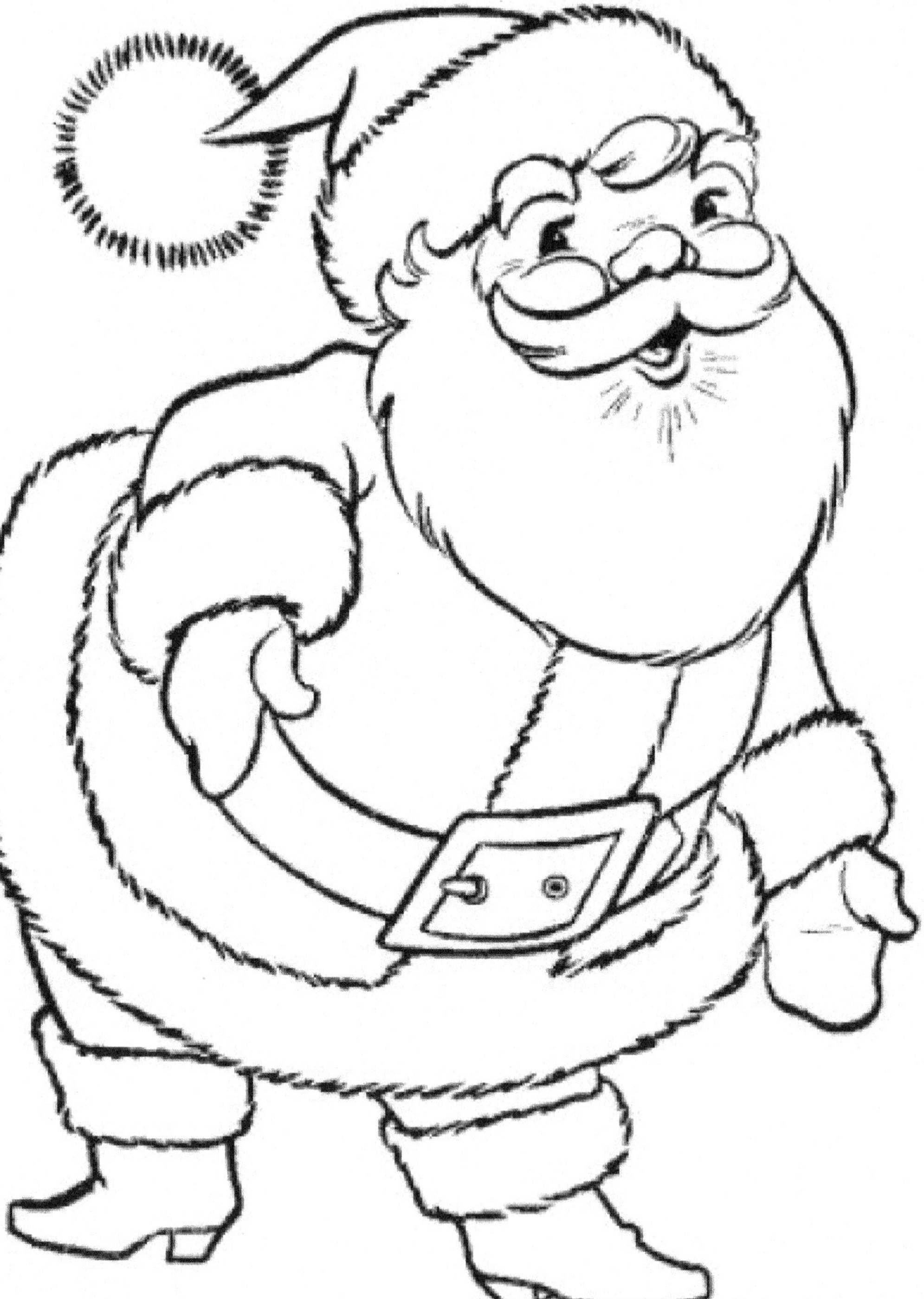

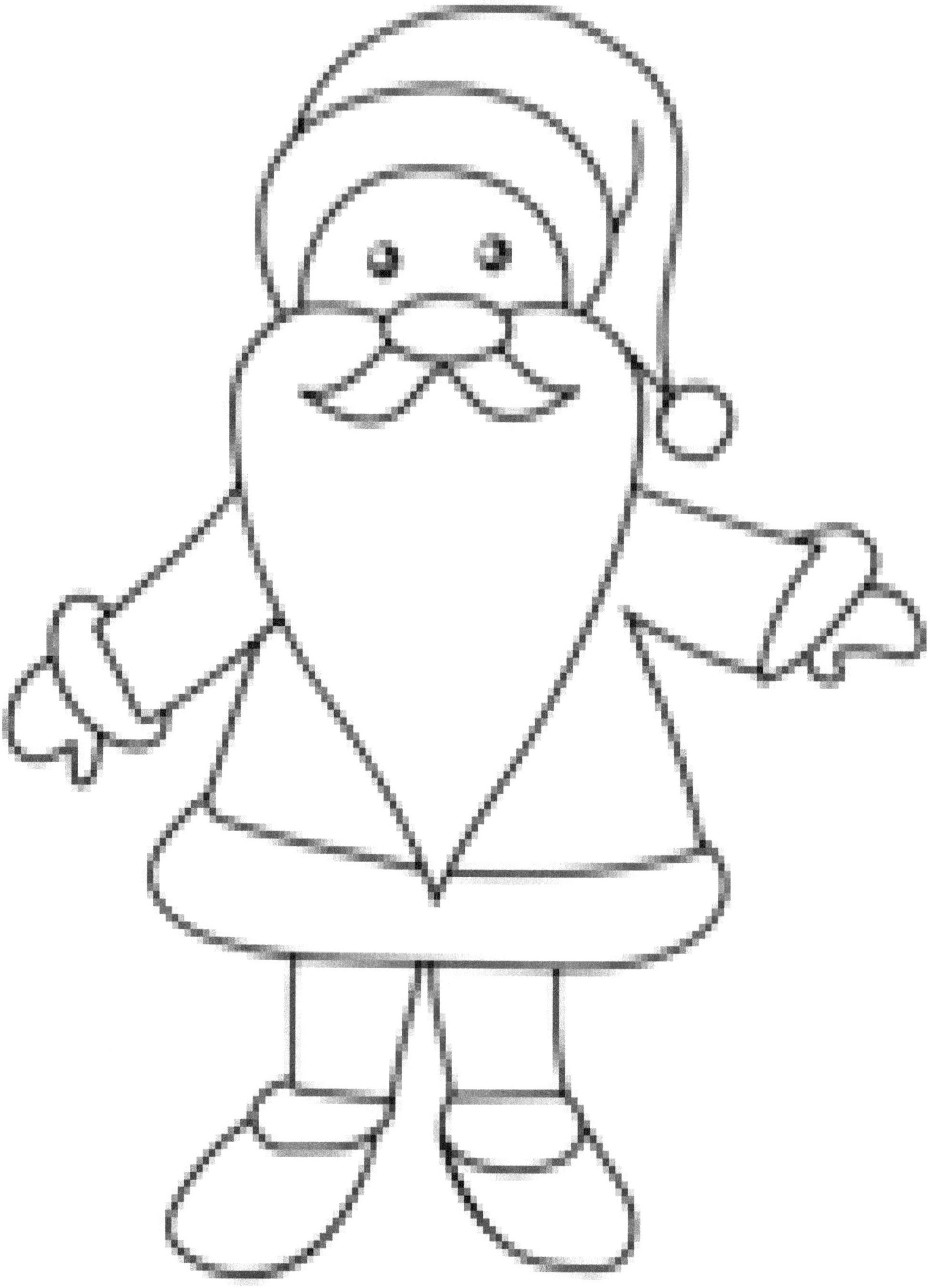

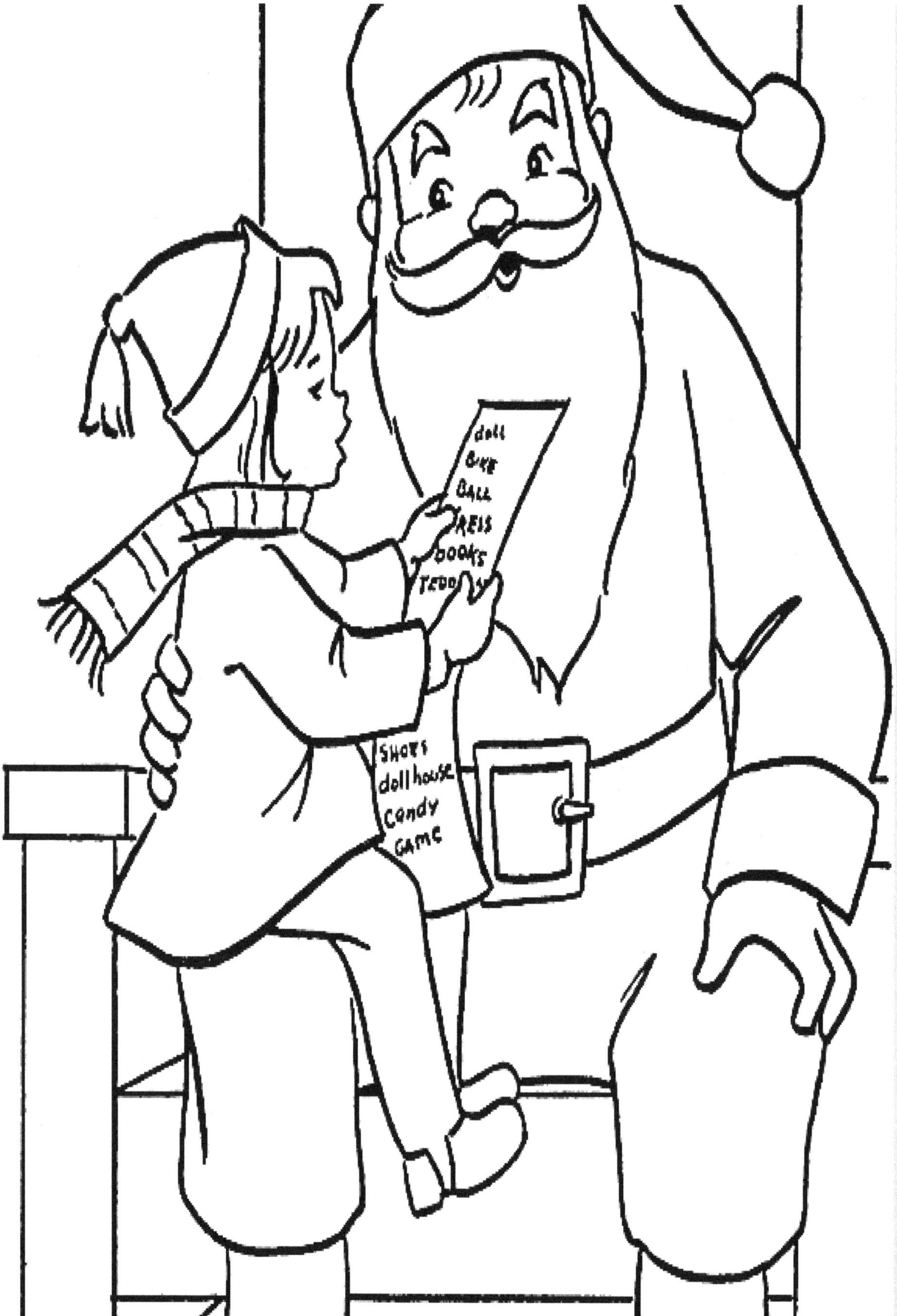
doll
BIKE
BALL
BOOKS
SHOES
doll house
candy
GAME

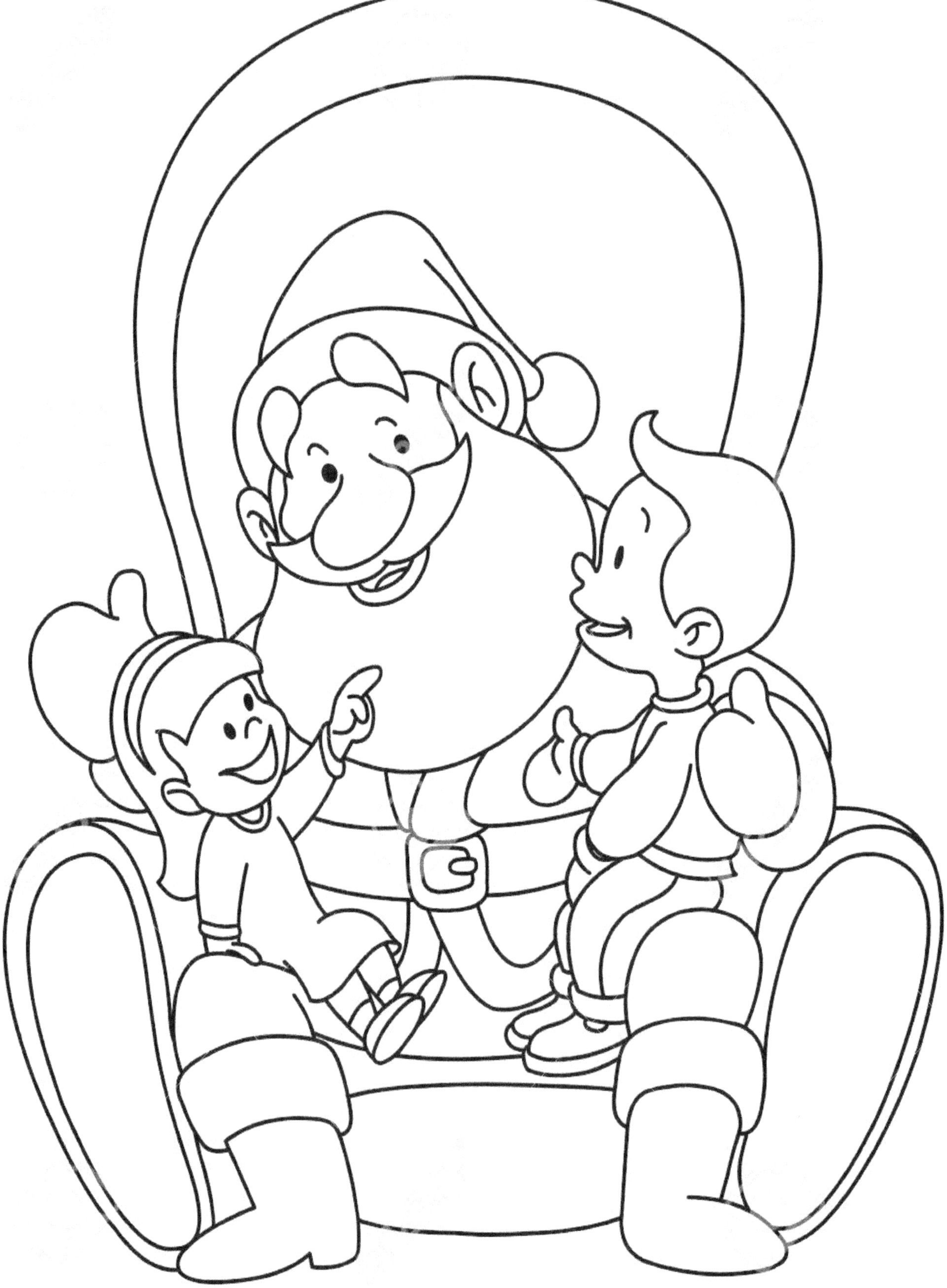

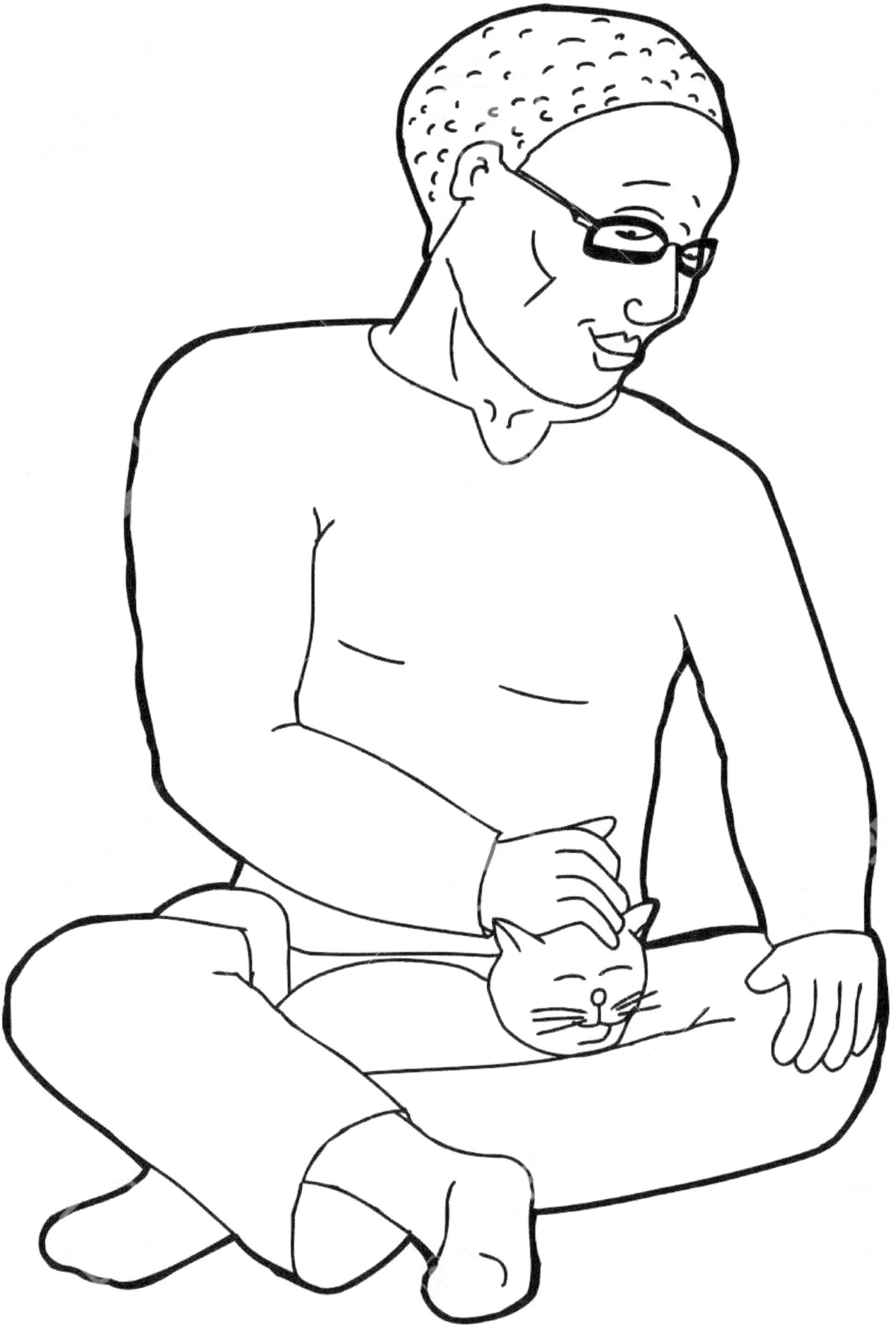

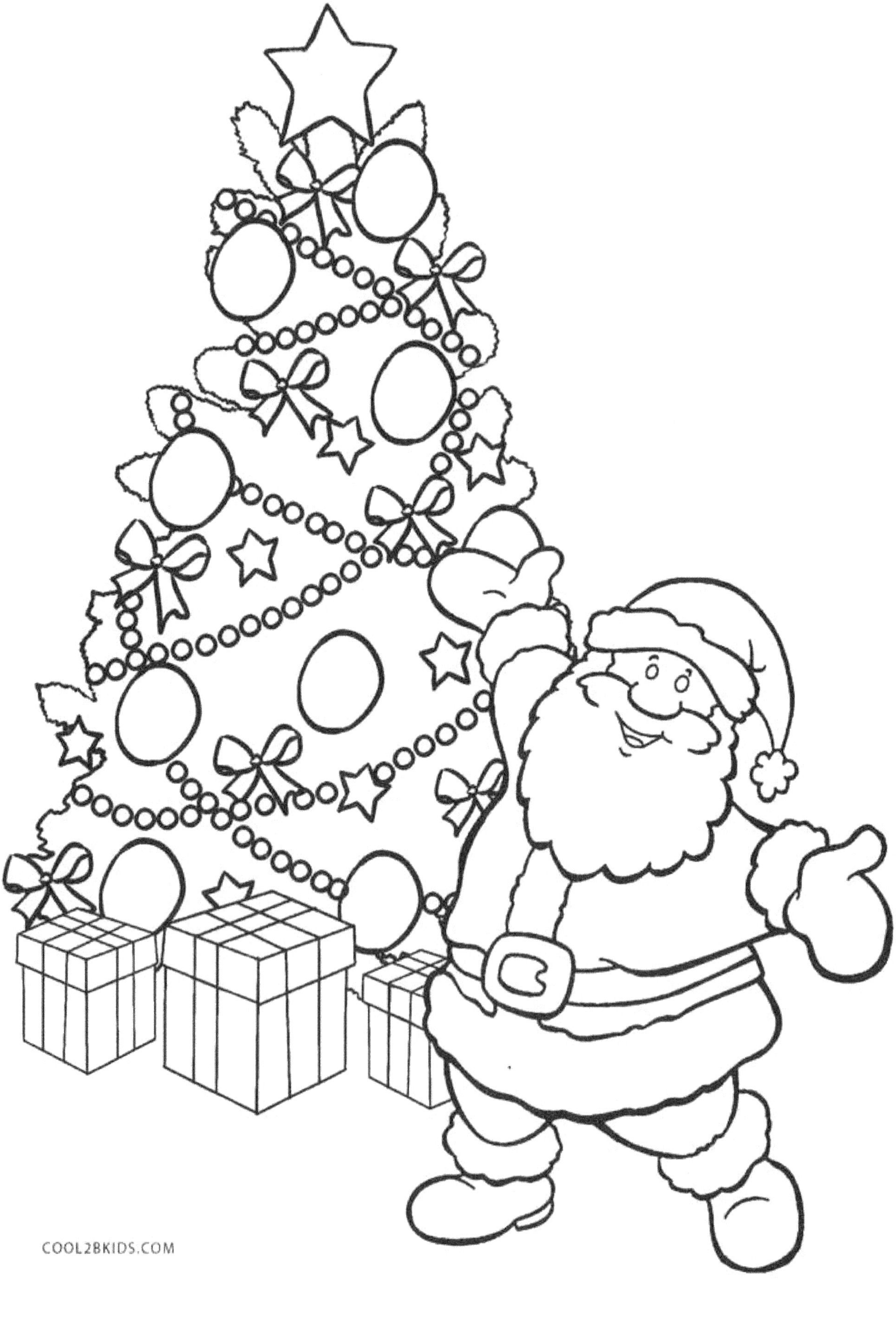

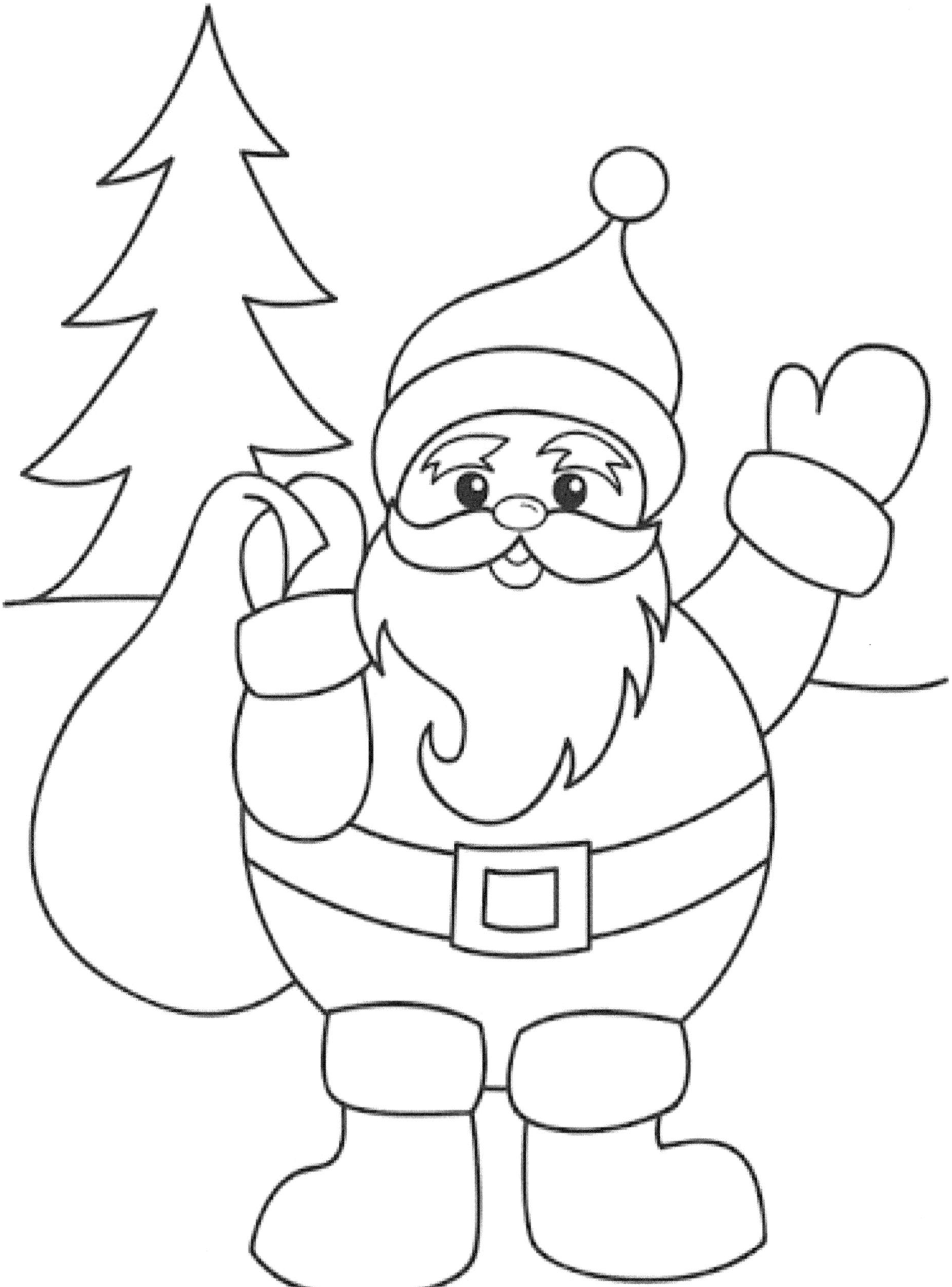

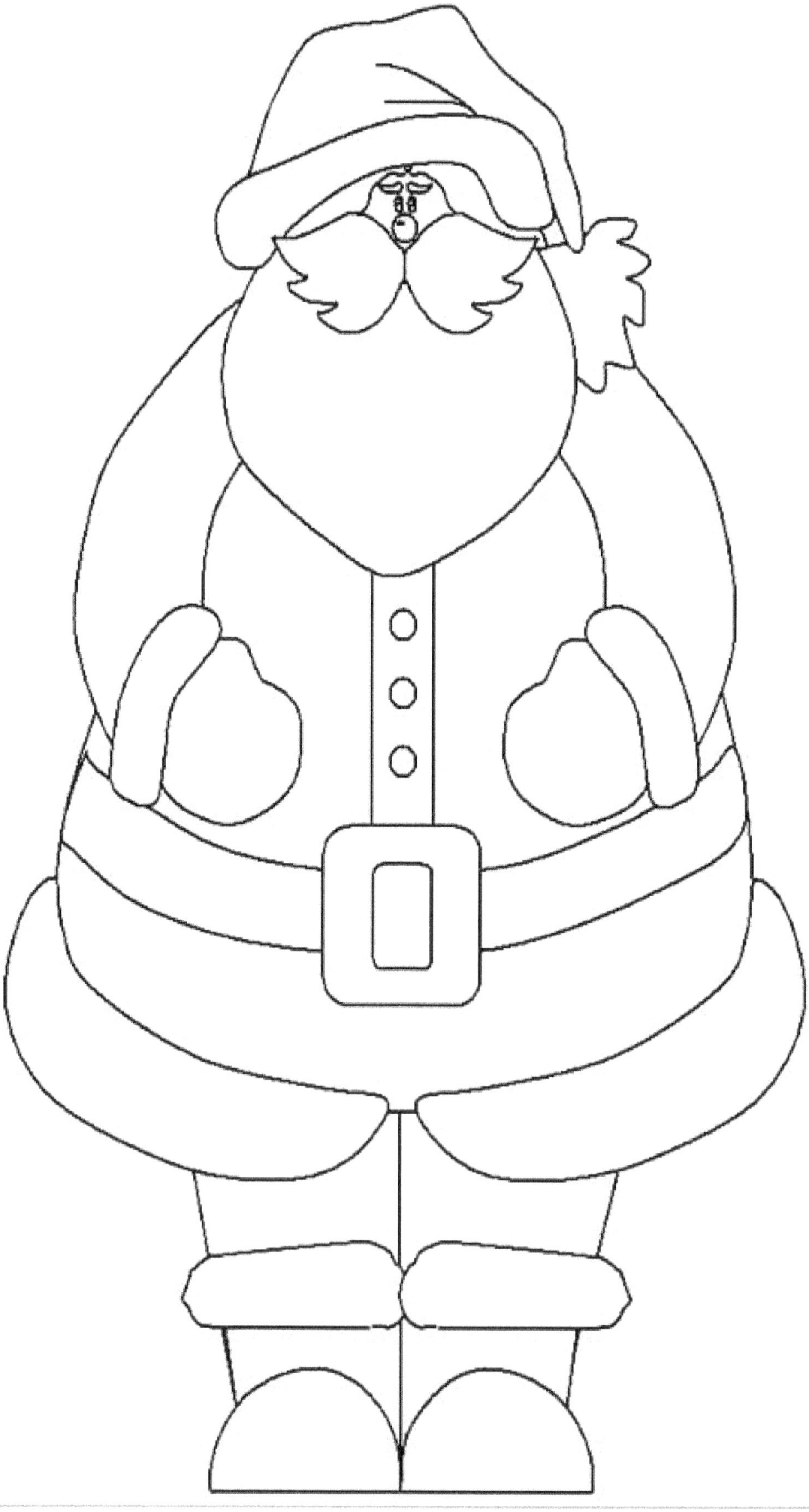

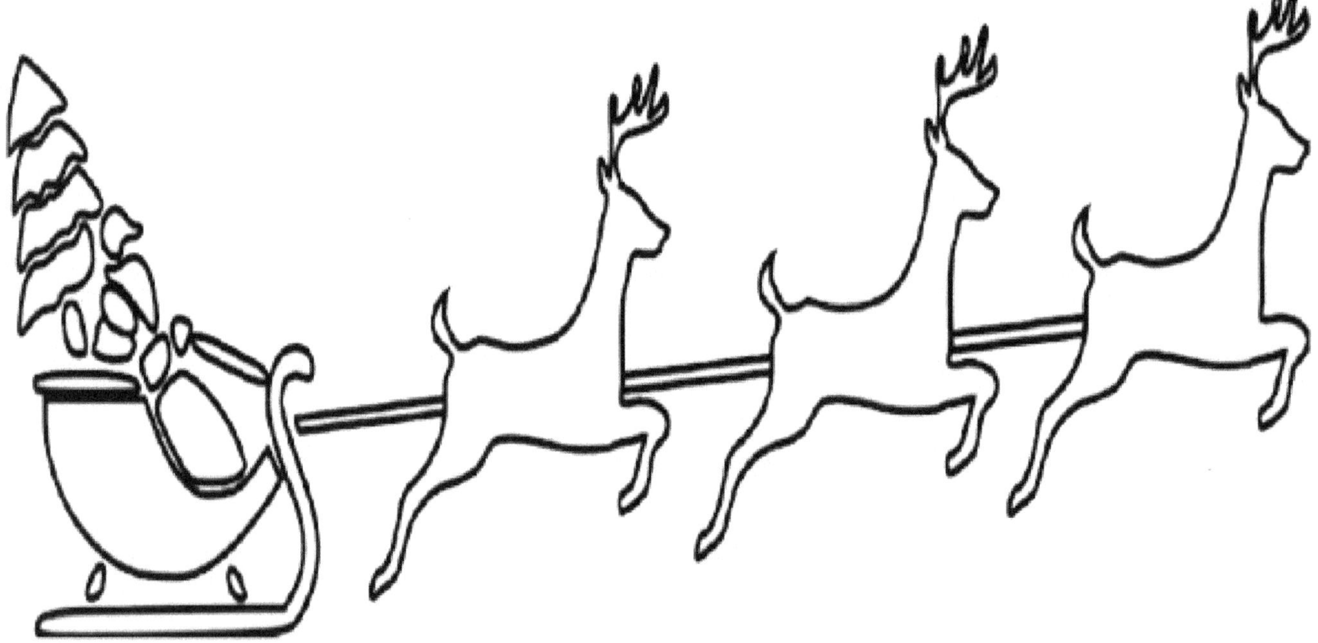

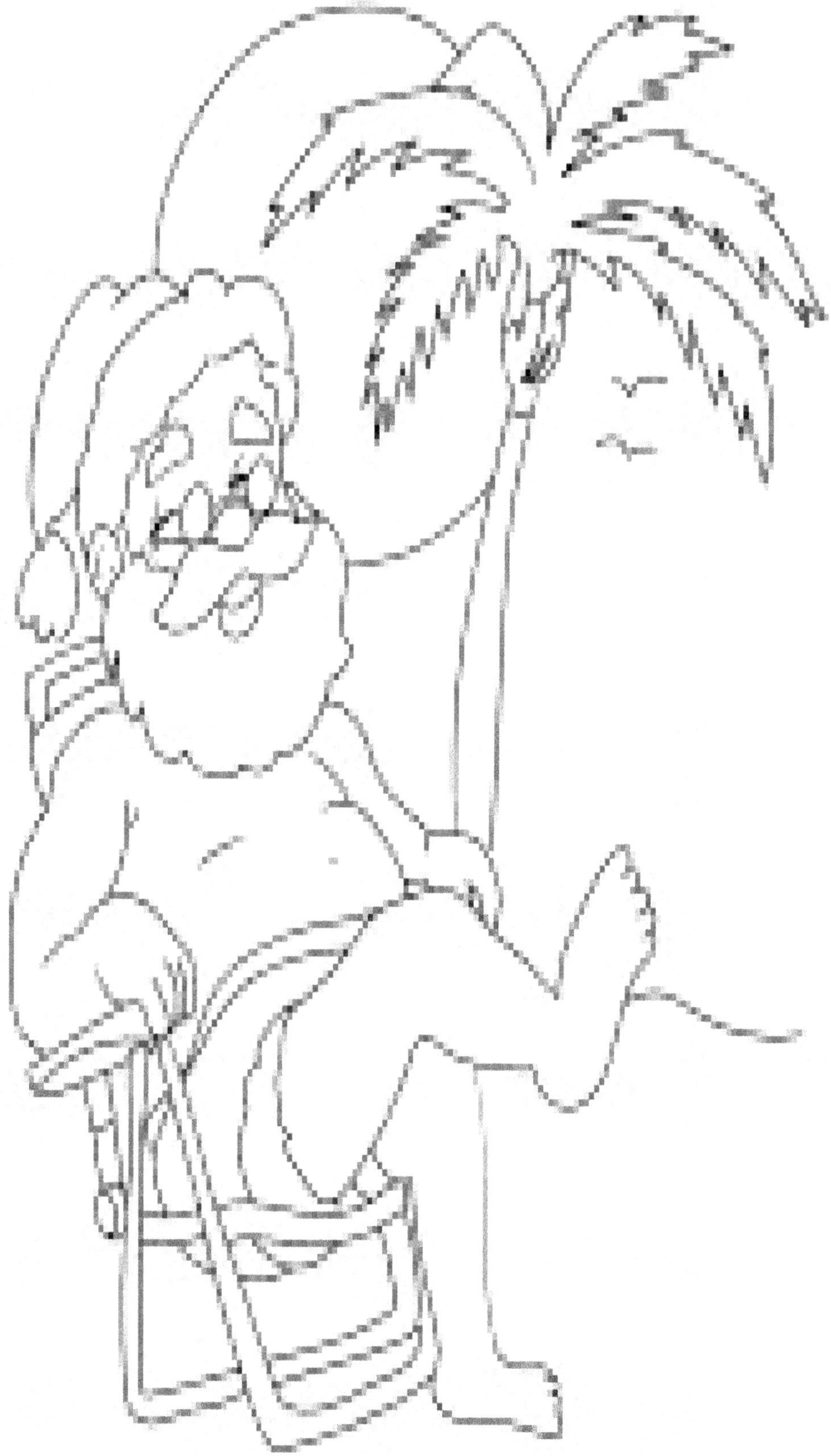

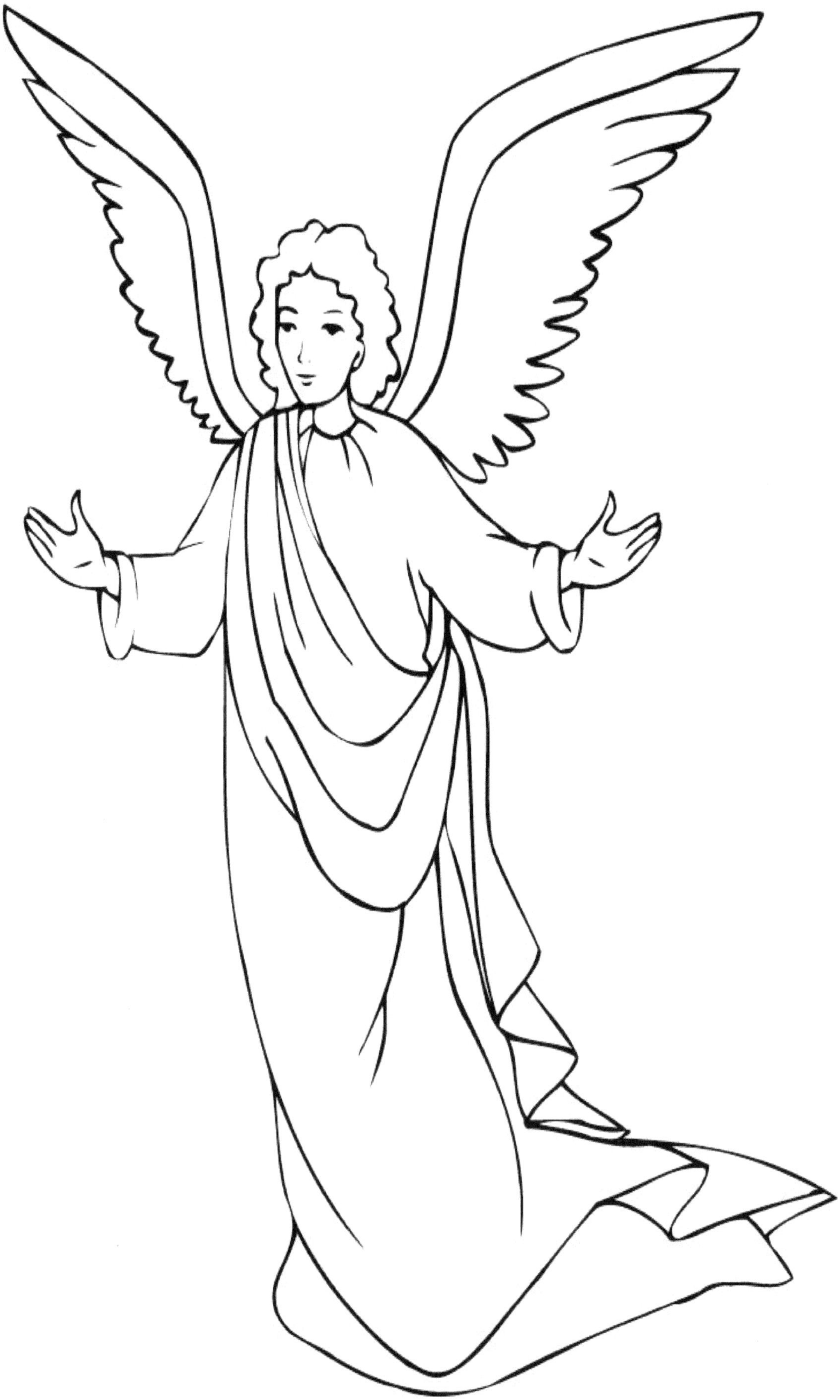

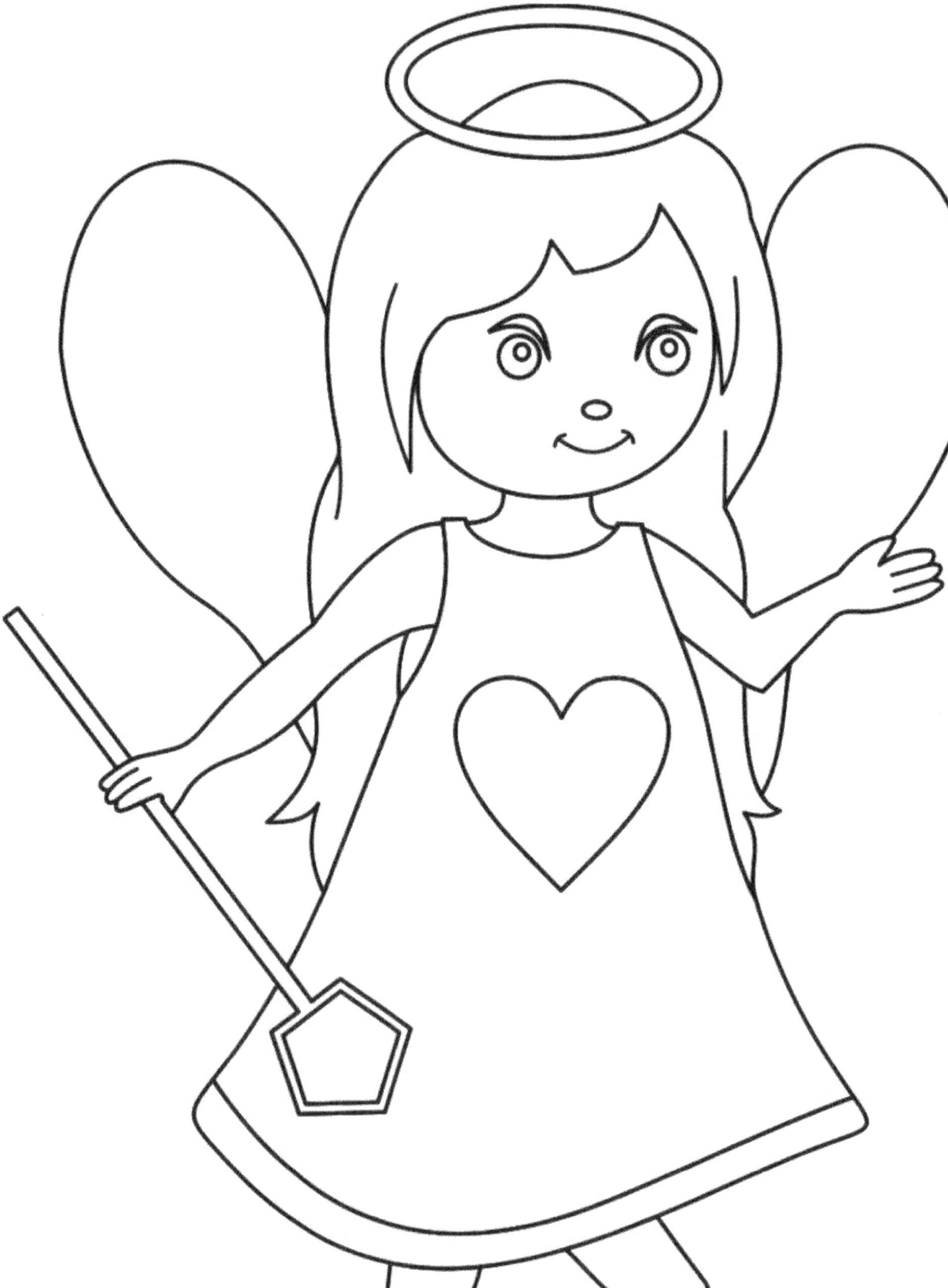

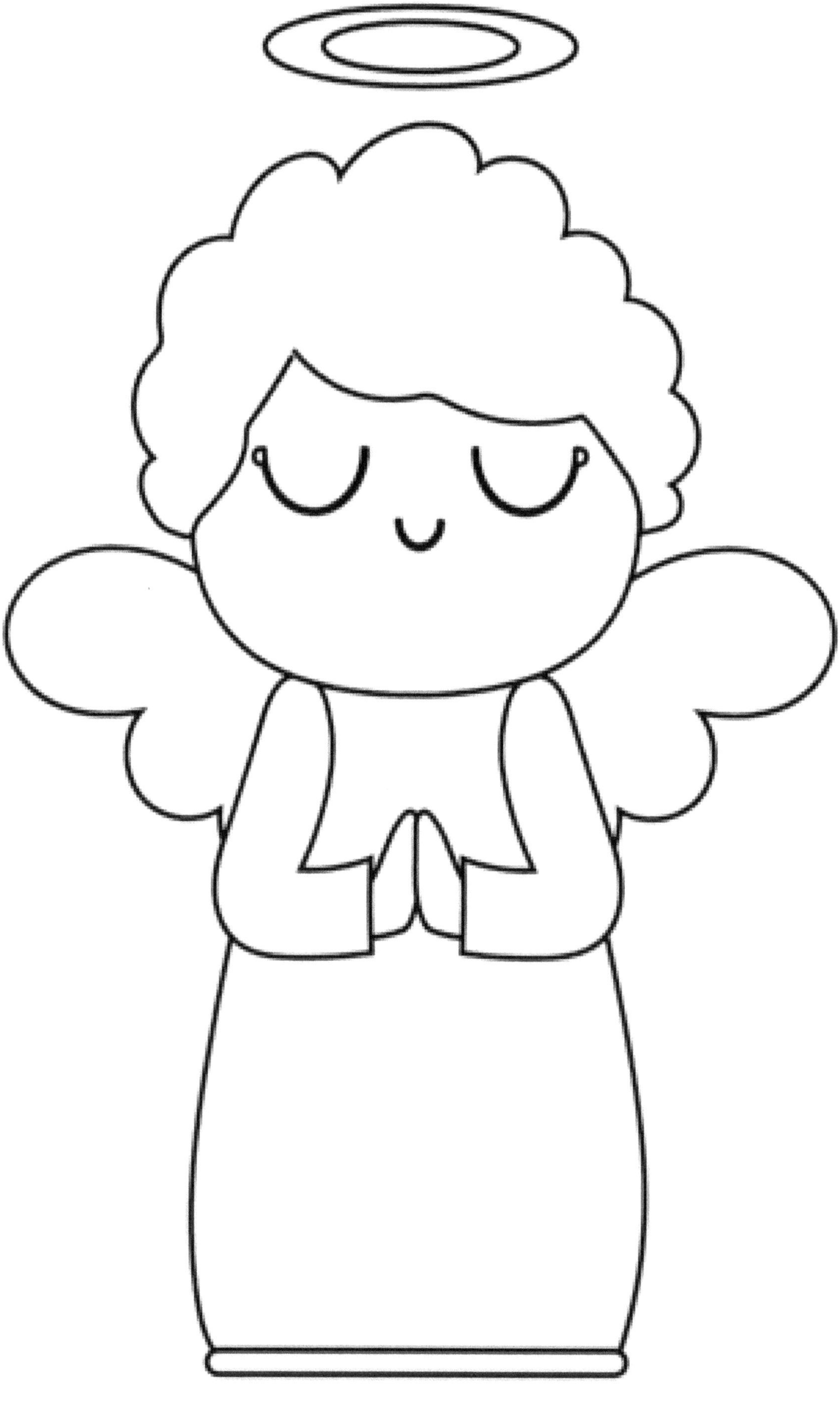

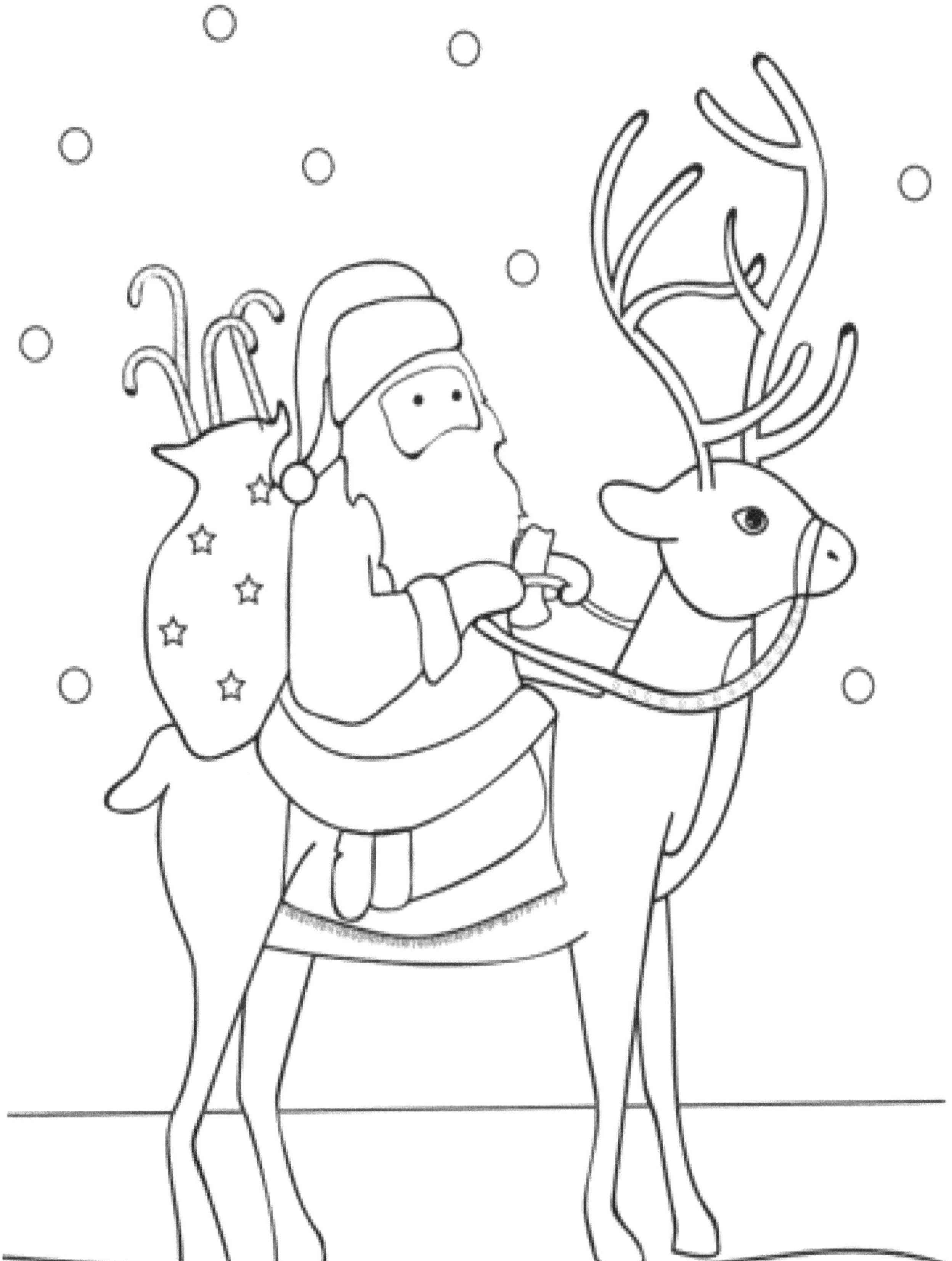

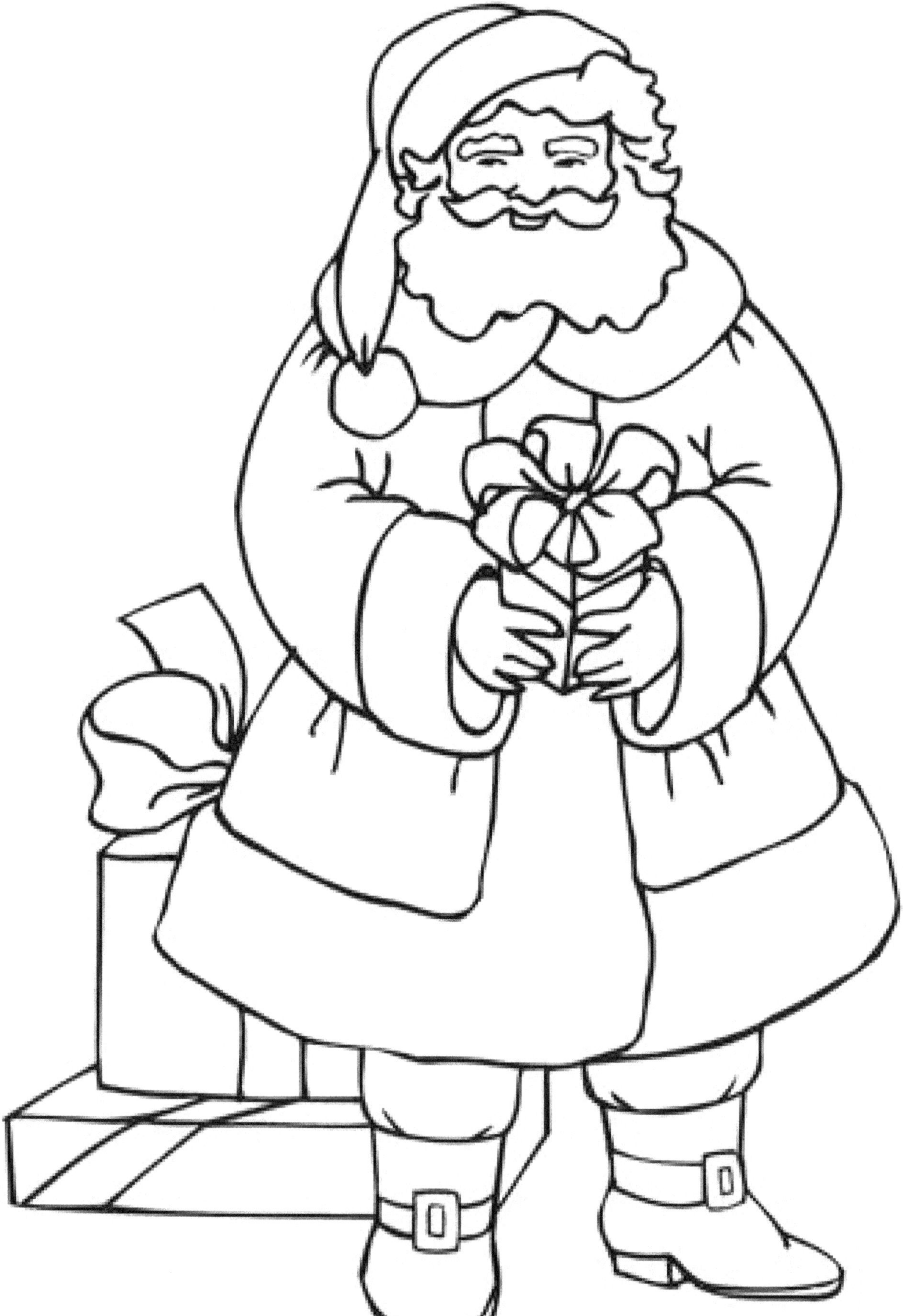

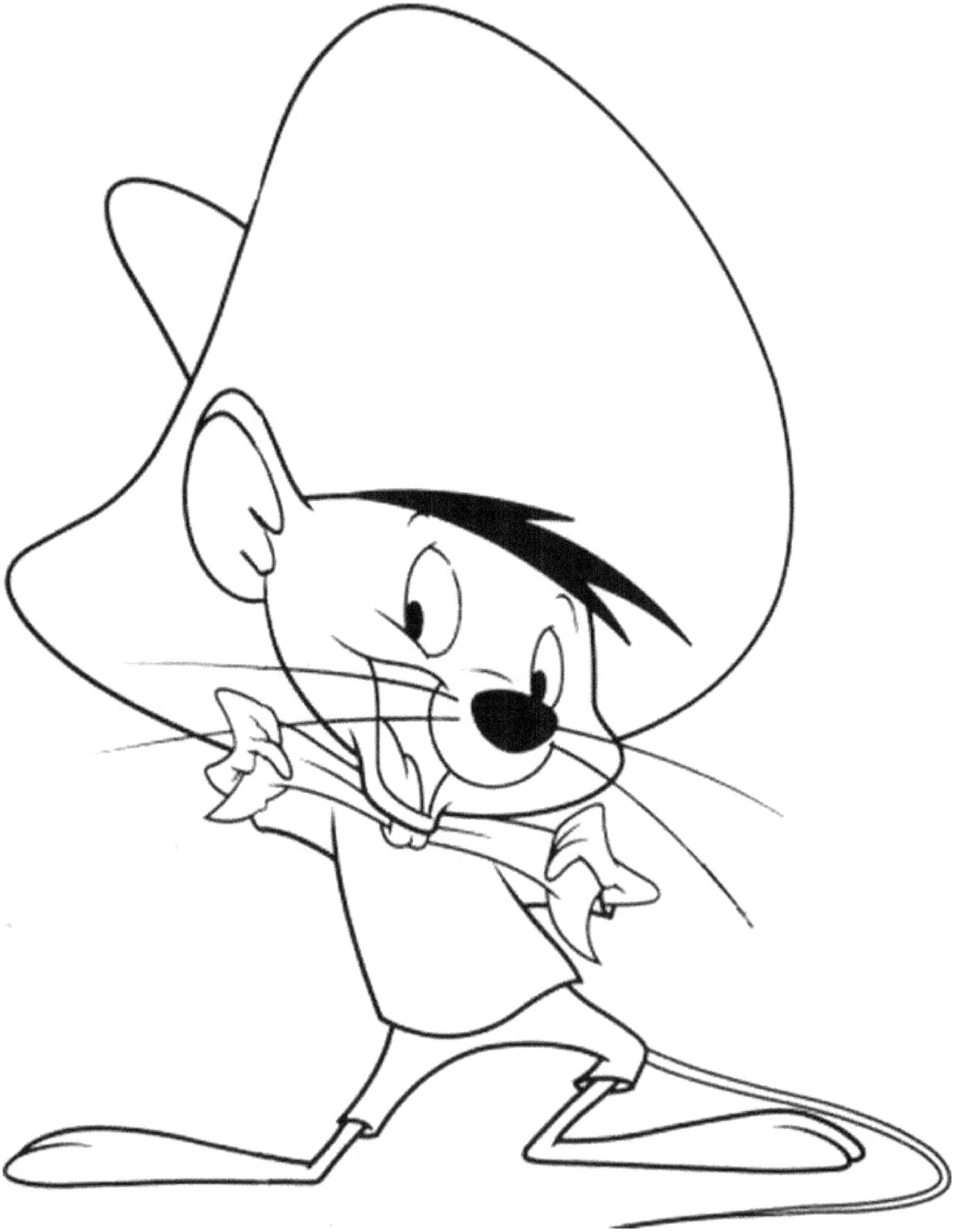

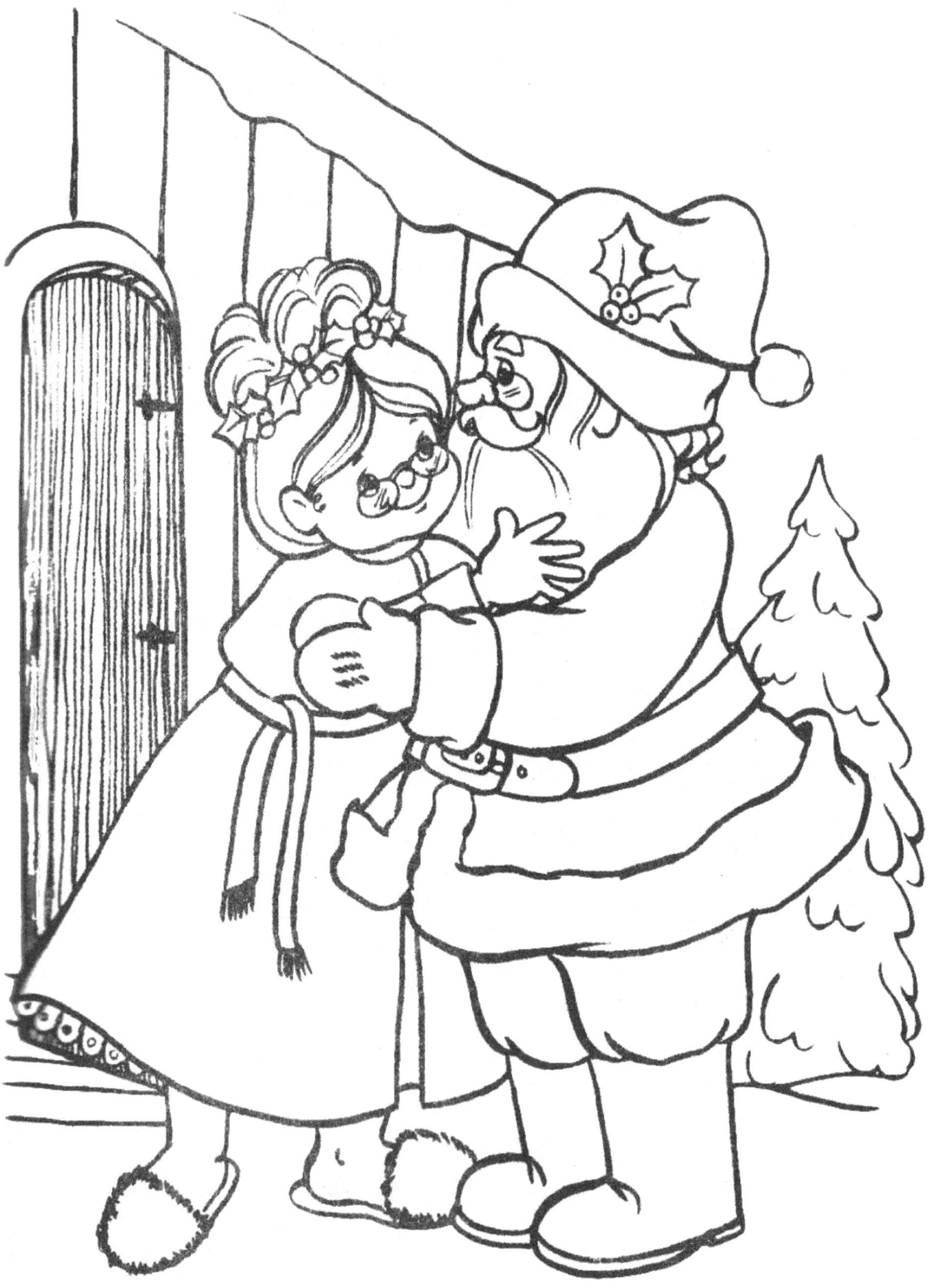

www.ingramcontent.com/pod-product-compliance
Lightning Source LLC
Chambersburg PA
CBHW081013201224
19312CB00044B/1072

9 798569 331413